Crouching Hidden Hogan: The Sixth Lesson

THE SECRET OF BEN HOGAN'S PERFECT AND AUTOMATIC GOLF SWING

Pradeep Bahirwani

Pradeep Bahirwani

RBB 808, Purva Riviera Apartments

Varthur Road, Marathahalli, Bangalore 560037

Karnataka, India

Email: author@crouchingtigerhiddenhogan.com

www.crouchingtigerhiddenhogan.com

Ordering Information:

Special discounts are available on quantity purchases by corporations, associations, and others. For details, contact the author at the address above.

Crouching Tiger Hidden Hogan: The Sixth Lesson / Pradeep Bahirwani —1st edition

ISBN: 978-1537365435

Contents

Dedicated to
Ben Hogan and Homer Kelley

Reverse every natural instinct and do the opposite of what you are inclined to do, and you will probably come very close to having a perfect golf swing.

BEN HOGAN (1912-1997)

Preface

THE GOAL OF THIS journey is on page eighty-five where the Perfect and Automatic swing is reduced to a single illustration and a simple instruction of five lines. But fast-forwarding the short distance from here to page eighty-five will not get you there because arrival at the destination without the rigor of the journey creates no transformation. It is my promise, however, that both the journey *and* the destination will be worth your while.

Like millions of golfers, I too was smitten by the charms of the game. It was love at first swing. And like a million golfers, I too bought a copy of the best-selling golf instruction book - Ben Hogan's *Five Lessons: The Modern Fundamentals of Golf*. I read it diligently from cover to cover. It is a thin little book with vivid images created by the renowned sports illustrator Anthony

Ravielli. Thus armed, I began to haunt the practice range with the zeal of the new disciple. It took a couple of years before the realization dawned on me: I could not swing like Mr. Hogan. The instruction in *Five Lessons* could not make me swing like Mr. Hogan. I looked around and found myself in august company. Nobody else has been able to swing like Mr. Hogan either.

In despair, I turned to other avenues, other swing methodologies. During the course of this process, I hit 5000 golf balls a month for five straight years. Each time I discovered a new way to hit a golf ball, I compared it to the Master's technique and said: "This is not the way Mr. Hogan hit the ball". Deep inside, without my being conscious of it, I had become a seeker of the Holy Grail of Golf. Such was the mesmerizing effect of the Master's fluid and powerful motion. The quest became an obsession with me. I researched everything I could find about the Master. As I gained insights into the life, times and the mind of the Master, I discovered the reason why *Five Lessons* could not help me duplicate his swing. It is called Hogan's Secret. It was in this way that I embarked on my quest for the Holy Grail.

Crouching Tiger, Hidden Hogan: The Sixth Lesson is the revelation of Hogan's Secret. But it is not intended to be a primary instruction book on his techniques. That position unquestionably belongs to *Five Lessons: The Modern Fundamentals of Golf.* So why read this book? First, it reveals the Secret. Second, it bridges the gaps that have so far held back golfers from successfully implementing the Master's methods. But the journey starts with *Five Lessons*. Golfers who have read that book will derive the maximum value out of this one.

Crouching Tiger, Hidden Hogan: The Sixth Lesson is based on the only theory *and* physical model that corroborates *everything* that the Master wrote and said and did. It is based on simple principles of physics and geometry and a startling fact of human bio-mechanics never published before in any medical or golf journal. A scaled down prototype of the physical model - the Body Swing Golfing Machine - is also the basis of my patent application.

The first part of the book, *Hidden Hogan,* is written as a story about the discovery of the Holy Grail. I hope it makes for a compelling reading experience for you. It certainly made for a wonderful writing experience for me. While there is the element of fiction in it, all the golfing details are scientific and validated. The second part, *Crouching Tiger,* derives the Master's fundamentals from the Secret and paves the way towards successful implementation and execution. A particular subset of technical golfers will find the additional material in the appendices interesting. Hogan aficionados will easily identify with the appendix covering Hoganisms: gaps between what the Master said and what he really meant.

The text and illustrations in this book refer to a right-handed golfer. I apologize to left-handed golfers in advance and humbly request that they reverse the interpretations as necessary.

I have enjoyed the process of digging the Master's Secret out of the dirt and presenting it to you in this book. I hope you too enjoy the process of discovering, understanding and applying the Master's Secret.

Pradeep Bahirwani

Book One:
Hidden Hogan

Prologue

HELLO. MY IDENTITY DOES not really matter, so please just call me Crouching Tiger. It is a generic term that Hiroki Kojiro coined to symbolize the faceless and average but reasonably coordinated golfer. Before I became Crouching Tiger, I was Racing Rat. That is a generic term *I* coined to symbolize the faceless and average but reasonably abled employee whose life revolves around office, meetings, e-mail, travel and promotions. I started my corporate career highly motivated by the motto: work is worship. But after two decades of working – or worshipping - I recognized that I was nowhere close to actualization, or by whatever other name one chooses to call God. And it was sometime later that the light of realization dawned on me. The fault lay not with the motto, but the chosen field of work. Actualization can be found in Truth, Goodness or Beauty but not in Commerce. Or to put it differently, God can be found in the pursuit of Science, Religion or Art but not in Business.

I am not a religious person. I have never been one. But Science and Art both appeal to me, and in Golf I found the ideal combination of both. Perfection is the highest attainment. It is mastery in all three dimensions: the physical, mental and spiritual. The journey through these dimensions is concurrent, but mastery must first be attained in the physical dimension, followed by the mental and spiritual in that order.

The earnest golfer and committed seeker will sooner or later run into Ben Hogan. He was the Master, the man who came closest to Perfection. It was thus that I began my quest for the Master's Perfect and Automatic swing. This is the story of my arrival at the first milestone.

After five years, ten thousand hours, permanent calluses, occasional tendonitis and an unhappy triggerfinger, Hiroki Kojiro showed up and this is what he told and showed me.

CHAPTER 1

The Sixth Lesson

I AM HIROKI KOJIRO. Please don't be alarmed, for my intention isn't hostile in the least. Besides, the war ended more than six decades ago. Here, shake my hand and be reassured. Warm flesh and blood, just like yours, no? Good, now there, thank you. But I quite understand your jumpiness. I would've felt the same had you accosted me out of the blue on this deserted golf course. How do I know your name? Never mind, for far more important is my purpose for being here. So let me explain.

I'm the founder of a secret group of golfers called the Hogan Circle. Though they call me the Master, we really have no pecking order. Neither do we have any clandestine rituals or hidden agenda. Besides, I'm not really comfortable with the term Master, because I believe there is only one Master and that is Ben Hogan, the greatest ball striker in the history of golf. Hoganites - as we like to call ourselves - are few in number but come from diverse backgrounds in profession, religion, gender, nationality and ethnicity. Each one has been carefully handpicked on the basis of attitude and a few other qualities, but golfing talent was not one of them. Like you, all of them were once average golfers. But knowledge of the Master's Secret – the Sixth Lesson - has turned them into single-digit handicappers. I have come to induct you into the Hogan Circle.

I have come to induct you into the Hogan Circle.

Why you? Well, I'm coming to that. Like all other Hoganites, you are desperate to play well. You have no shortage of commitment, but success at this enigmatic game eludes you. You love to practice and experiment as much as you love to play. You value golf for inner growth, not external approval or material gain. We've been watching you for quite some time now. We've observed your untiring effort, day after day and year after year, to duplicate the Master's swing. The Hogan Circle has done its homework on you. Your time has come. You're ready now for the Sixth Lesson. But our interest in you runs deeper. That's the reason *I* am here *in person* before you, even though all Hoganites are equally capable of delivering the Sixth Lesson.

Let me clarify. The Master believed in the journey, the process of discovery, the digging of dirt. It took the Master twenty three years of hard work and doggedness to discover the Secret. Now take your example. You've done five years of digging– relentlessly– I must say – but can you keep it up for another eighteen years? Do you realize the enormity of the task that you've undertaken? The average golfer simply doesn't have the time and energy to practice given the pace and pressures of modern life. Neither does he have the proper instruction to accelerate his progress towards his goal. Many golfers have deserted the game because they have found it too difficult to master. Unfortunately, their number is growing by the day. The Master regarded Golf as a game invented by the highest inspiration in humankind. It would've pained him immeasurably to see the crisis in the game today.

The Hogan Circle is the custodian of the Master's Secret. We've researched, refined and expanded it into a comprehensive and scientific body of knowledge. It's for the greater good of the game that the Hogan Circle has decided to share this knowledge without qualification or discrimination. In a way, as we'll see, this'll also be a completion of the Master's unfinished agenda. The

Hogan Circle has chosen you to write the book that reveals the Master's Secret to the golfing world.

Why you? You're that elusive combination of engineer, artist, writer and golfer *and* Hogan devotee. But, my friend, it would be better if you let me do the talking and keep the questions to a minimum. We've just this evening and I have a lot to share with you. Good, it seems we have an understanding. Now, let's walk over to the clubhouse.

To share the Master's Secret with you, I'll have to take you briefly through the values and beliefs of the Hogan Circle. Some of what I've to say in this regard may already be known to you, but I still request you to listen carefully. If nothing else, it'll serve to validate that we speak the same language as you.

Golf is a game of continuous evolution, not instant transformation. There is a trinity of dimensions in the game of golf – the physical, mental and spiritual. Three is a special number to us in more ways than one. You see this symbol here in the back of my cap? What do you make of it? Ah, yes, three concentric circles, something like a target in archery, you say? But look closer. Notice that the circles are asymmetric in their distances to the common center? But the casual observer may be forgiven for not noticing. It was meant to be discreet. The three concentric circles is the symbol of the Hogan Circle for good reason, as we'll discover.

I'm a martial arts practitioner and teacher. My specialization is swordsmanship. I'm also a calligraphist and an advanced student of Zen techniques, but still nowhere close to the Master who had attained the highest level. The energy around the Master had an unbelievable physical presence. People flocked around from near and far just to watch him at practice hitting ball after ball for hours at end. Somebody has likened the experience to being in church. That's the unmistakable aura around a Zen Master.

Physical mastery entails acquiring and developing the proper techniques. You can only do this in the practice range. Practice is the repetition of a single motion with the goal of mastering it. But Hoganites spend an equal amount of time, if not more, in experimenting. We experiment with a view to improve the Master's techniques, we try out new things, we discard things that do not work and retain things that do. Any new technique or variation is validated by other Hoganites over a period of months before it is accepted into our growing body of knowledge.

The mental and spiritual aspects of golf are vast topics of discussion in themselves, and will altogether take much more time than we have today. Therefore let's talk about the physical aspect only. That is where it all started for the Master when he made his first breakthrough. The Secret was God's gift and the Master used it well, but not as well as he *could* have. He used it as a tool for *his* evolution all right, but he believed that anyone who wished to evolve likewise had to work equally hard for *theirs*. It turns out that the true test of evolution is not: how much did you evolve? Rather, it is: how many did you help evolve?

The unfinished agenda of sharing the Secret for this greater cause is now for you to complete. Do you realize the amount of trust the Hogan Circle has placed in you? Do you feel the responsibility that you must shoulder? And you have just this evening to assimilate it. Don't worry, I'll explain it all. While I certainly desire you to be faithful to my *word*, you do have artistic license in the matter of recording what I show and tell you. What is of more importance is the guiding *spirit* behind it.

The Master's pitch to his publisher was: "I've finally got the fundamentals of the golf swing worked out so clearly in my own mind that I'm certain any reasonably coordinated golfer who applies them can shoot in the 70s". I like to put it a little bit differently:

THERE IS A CROUCHING TIGER WAITING TO BE UN-LEASHED INSIDE EVERY GOLFER. THE LEASH IS KNOWLEDGE, NOT POTENTIAL. KNOWLEDGE OF THE MASTER'S SECRET IS THE KEY TO UNLEASH THAT PO-TENTIAL.

CHAPTER 2

The Hogan Code

AH, HERE WE ARE at the clubhouse at last. Let's sit in that corner over there. Yes, this is perfect. It's quiet and likely to remain that way. Kindly allow me to make the choice of food and drink, please. I don't usually impose myself upon my host like this, but today's an exceptional circumstance, you agree? Good, let's start off with a vodka martini. They don't serve vodka back where I come from. Can you hail the waiter please?

They say that the Master's swing is the most studied athletic action in the history of sport. But that wasn't so when he started out to play professional golf. He realized that he didn't have the finest swing out there, and therefore he decided to practice twice as hard to beat the guys who *did*. He did his best to figure out what they were doing and to learn from them. But it took two decades for the Master to evolve his own swing, one that suited his body and temperament.

The golf swing is a complex thing. A number of components must fall in place before the motion functions like clockwork. The swing becomes dysfunctional even if one component is wrong, is missing or is simply out of place. I'm talking about components that are unique to every individual's physical makeup. For example, the way your elbow bends, or your wrist hinges, or the point of balance of your body and its axis of rotation.

By the early forties, the Master was winning tournaments but he knew that he was well short of physical mastery. He was still on the quest for the Perfect and Automatic swing. When he did make the breakthrough, it appeared to the world at large that he had undergone an instant transformation from average to excellent ball striker. But people didn't see the two decades of continuous search and experimentation that he went through before it all clicked into place.

The Master was a modest man. Self-doubt came easy to him. But he recognized it when he got it. That swing was a phenomenal sensation. The impact sounded like a rifle shot. His confidence in the Secret was one thousand percent, not one hundred percent. The Master therefore relaxed his practice after that, but he continued to experiment to further refine his technique. In fact, he experimented and practiced long after he gave up playing professional golf.

At first the Master toyed with the idea of completely revamping his swing. To make such a big change on the fly is a very difficult proposition. You have to keep in mind that he had to show up week after week, at tournament after tournament, and win as much as he could to make a living. But what sealed the deal was the realization that the ideal, Secret-driven swing would be a dead giveaway to the trained eye. His rivals on the Tour would have picked it up in a jiffy. That thought simply consumed him; it made him paranoid. The Master never went to business school but he instinctively grasped the concept of competitive advantage. In golf a competitive advantage is a superior technique that cannot be easily duplicated by rivals.

So the Master retained the big lateral move of his old swing, even though it had become redundant. It worked. His competitors never did quite catch on. That shaped his attitude for the rest of his lifetime. The subtler the change the better is the disguise, the lesser the talk the deeper is the mystique, the broader the hint the safer is the Secret.

So that's the reason why copying the Master's positions isn't the best way to search for his Secret. The Master's swing, the post-Secret swing that everyone studies is a transitional one. It's different from his old swing but still well short of the purely rotational, Secret-driven swing. But once you discover the Master's principle, you can find your own way to make it work for you.

THE TRUTH SETS US FREE. THE MASTER'S SECRET LIBERATES US FROM HAVING TO IMITATE HIM. ONCE WE DISCOVER THE SECRET, WE CAN APPLY THE MASTER'S PRINCIPLE INSTEAD OF HAVING TO DUPLICATE HIS POSITIONS.

The Master's Secret is simple. It's conceptually the simplest solution to the central problem in golf. That's, of course, if you can recognize and define this problem clearly. The Secret is in full and plain view of the world all the time, but nobody discerns it because it's present neither at the start of the Master's swing nor at the end but somewhere in between.

Because the Master's Secret is a particular application of a general principle, there are many ways of implementing it. But all of them have one thing in common - the Hogan Code, which works like a key that unlocks the vault of the Holy Grail. This code, known only to Hoganites, is a combination of numbers that arise directly out of the Master's Secret. It can't be arrived at by guesswork, but a golfer who has thoroughly understood the Master's principle will find it relatively simple to crack. How's that? The Master left specific clues in his book but they were cryptic and buried in the rest of the print.

The Hogan Code arises directly out of the Master's Secret.

THE HOGAN CODE IS A SPECIFIC COMBINATION OF FOUR NUMBERS EACH OF WHICH REPRESENTS A CRUCIAL ELEMENT WITHOUT WHICH THE SWING WILL NOT WORK. THESE NUMBERS ARE WRITTEN IN THE ORDER THAT THEY ARE USED IN THE SWING. THE HOGAN CODE IS:

$$AX\text{-}BX\text{-}CX\text{-}DX$$

A, B, C and D are integers and X is a measurement with both magnitude and units. AX and BX are setup attributes; CX and DX are movement attributes. Don't be dissuaded by this string of numbers - the Hogan Code is simple and symmetrical in concept and like clockwork in execution.

After we are through with the Sixth Lesson, you'll be put to the test of decrypting the Hogan code. If you don't crack it, this entire exercise will become futile, meaningless. If you do pass the test, however, it'll tell me that you've understood the Secret and can reveal it to the world with clarity.

Are the integers A, B, C and D unique and mutually exclusive? That's a good question my friend, but one that I am afraid I'll not answer. It'll be your job to figure that out. But don't be afraid, all the information will be forthcoming. You'll have to distill it into knowledge, though. So pay close attention to what I'm going to show and tell you.

The Hogan Circle must set the record straight on this. The Master never lied to anyone about the Secret. People got this impression because he gave different hints to different people. To some he made oblique hints because he just wanted them off his back. But to the deserving he made broad and direct hints and left it to them to dig further and put together the puzzle. The

Master can therefore be faulted for not sharing the full truth, but not for telling the outright lie. The Master often toyed with people about the Secret by referring to a certain Henny Bogan as if it were his *alter ego*. It was in fact his *alter ego*, the one that gave him a fresh lease of life and the phenomenal success of his later career. Henny Bogan was the Master's Secret.

I think I'll have a repeat of the vodka martini. Can you do the honors please?

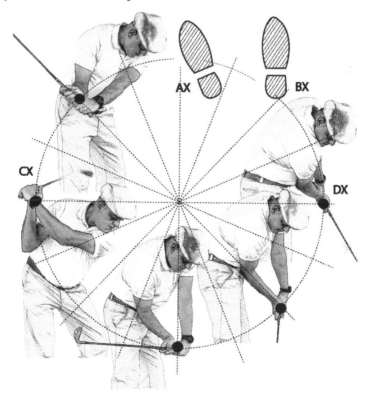

The Hogan Code is simple and symmetrical in concept and like clockwork in execution.

CHAPTER 3

Henny Bogan
Take One

WE WILL PUT TOGETHER Henny Bogan on paper, piece by piece, right here at this table. Here's a quick and dirty sketch. I'm afraid it'll have to do in the interest of saving time. You and I have a lot of ground to cover. I'm sure that you'll do a better job of reproducing it. This may seem like a bizarre contraption at first, but I can assure you that it's a formidable golfing machine. Let's just call it Henny Bogan Take One for now. You recognize the Hollywood jargon? Of course you do. The term 'Take' is used in Hollywood to represent and track the stages of production. We'll use it to track the steps in our development of Henny Bogan. As you're beginning to see, the Secret is technical in nature. But technology is par for the course in the game today. You have ball-flight radars, slow-motion video analysis, swing jackets and all manner of swing aids. It's completely a separate issue, though, that the average handicap hasn't reduced despite this proliferation of technology. It's got to do with problem definition, the separation of cause from symptom. But I digress, let me come back. In comparison to the technology in the game today, the technical details of Henny Bogan will appear rudimentary to you. Relax but pay attention; and let me take you through the journey from the Genesis of Henny Bogan to its full blown Resurrection.

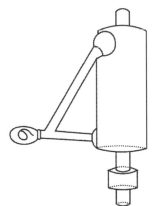

Henny Bogan Take One: a first look at the most formidable and exclusive golfing machine in the history of the game.

The Genesis of Henny Bogan dates back to 1946. At the age of thirty-four, the Master was already past his athletic prime. He was winning tournaments all right, but he lacked the confidence that comes from being at the top of one's game. He was struggling with his nemesis, the dreaded hook. Despite all the endless hours of practice he had put in, the hook would show up at the most inopportune of times and cause his downfall. The fact was of very little consolation that the better player fights the hook while the less accomplished player struggles with a slice.

The Master had run out of options. But he had to face the reality of the situation. So he quit the Tour for a few months and went home to figure a way out. He thought about it for a long time. The golf swing requires timing between the arms and the body. The arms go up and down but the body goes around. It requires athletic ability to synchronize the linear force exerted by the up-and-down motion of the arms with the rotational force exerted by the turning body. Even for the most athletic golfers, this timing is thrown off under pressure and results in all sorts of errors. This is the central problem of golf.

THE COMPLEXITY IN THE GOLF SWING ARISES FROM THE SYNCHRONIZING OF THE ARM SWING WITH THE TURN OF THE BODY. THIS REQUIRES ARM-BODY TIMING AND IS THE CENTRAL PROBLEM OF GOLF.

The Master knew very well that he was not the most talented golfer of his times. There were others who possessed this knack of timing and swung with more grace and fluidity than him. He realized that he had to figure out a way of taking the issue of arm-body timing out of the equation. It was like one of those celebrated thought experiments that Einstein did. The Master never went to college but his IQ has been estimated at 175, a full 15 points above the genius level. The Master was brilliant, introverted and left-brained. What do you think such a professional golfer would come up with when faced with a survival issue - a repeatable way to hit a golf ball long and accurate? What else but a machine, of course?

There is no getting away from the arm swing because it is the arms and hands that hold onto the club and cause it to move. The question therefore is the extent of body participation. What if the arm swing is made completely independent of the body? What if the arm swing is made completely dependent on the body? The Master experimented with these two extreme scenarios. They created two images in his mind. The first image was a completely vertical swing plane where the arms alone create the circle of the swing. The Master rejected this possibility because such a swing would work for the short clubs but not for the longer clubs because they needed to be moved on a flatter plane. Besides, given the three dimensional degrees of freedom of the shoulder joints it would be very difficult to keep the club on plane with the arms only. The second image was a flatter swing plane with the rotation of the body alone creating the circle of the golf swing. The Master went deeper into his thought experiment.

THE ARMS CAN SWING IN AN INFINITE NUMBER OF WAYS. BUT THE BODY CAN TURN ONLY IN ONE WAY AROUND A CENTRAL AXIS OF ROTATION.

It was this fact that predisposed the Master to the second image. The nature of the body turn is rotational. If the arm swing has to be in sync with the body turn at all times, the arms have to move in circular motion *around* the body. Such a motion should indeed be possible by shoulder rotation around the spinal axis. In a circular arm swing it would have to be the right arm that would play the key role. This is because the right arm can go around the body but the left arm stays in front of it. Moreover, it is the left arm that elevates the hands independent of body rotation in the concluding stage of the backswing. The Master therefore correctly concluded that the right arm would have to play the dominant role in transporting the club in sync with the body turn while the elevating action of the left arm would have to be suppressed.

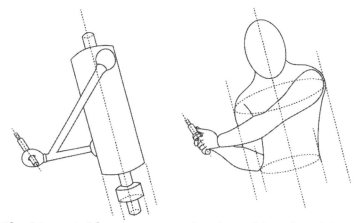

The Master's idea was a rotational machine that drives a connected and passive right-forearm into impact.

That is when the Master recalled the observations he had made by studying the swing of baseball players who used torso rotation to accelerate the arm swing. They planted their weight on the left side, connected the right elbow to the right side and rotated the right forearm around the spinal axis through impact. The Master could readily see the advantage of a right-arm swing with a connected right elbow constrained to move on a set path around the right side. That was similar to the action he had in mind. But the baseball swing was on a near horizontal plane. How could one adapt that to the golf swing which happened on an inclined plane?

That problem statement itself suggested the solution. The motion would be exactly the same except that the spinal axis would need to be tilted downwards to allow for the ball position on the ground. Henny Bogan was conceived at that precise moment: the Master's idea of a rotational machine that drives a connected and passive right-forearm into impact. It was a generic machine equipped with a chuck into which a variable tool could be fitted. In golf, the club is the tool. In baseball, the bat is the tool. But the swing, the action, remains the same. The difference is the plane in which the action happens. In baseball the action happens on a plane that passes through the hips and is parallel to the ground. In golf the action happens on a plane that again passes through the hips but is inclined with respect to the ground.

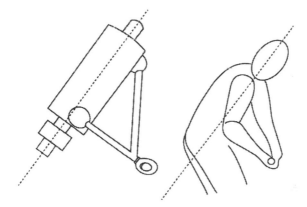

The basic motion of the machine is the same irrespective of the tilt of the axis of rotation.

THE MACHINE PROMISED COMPLETE LIBERATION FROM ARM-BODY TIMING AND SWING PLANE ERRORS. A MACHINE HAS NO SLACK, NO TOLERANCE OR MARGIN OF ERROR. SUCH A MACHINE WOULD HAVE A PERFECT AND AUTOMATIC SWING.

It was a singular leap of imagination. The concept of the machine liberated the Master from monitoring the plane of the club shaft just as the concept of the plane had liberated him from monitoring the arc of the club head.

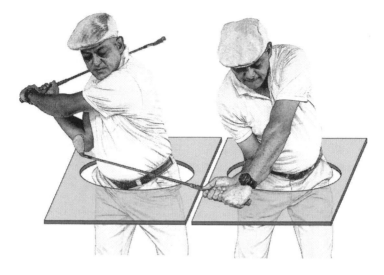

The connected shape of Henny Bogan returns the hands a little higher and a little from inside but in the same fashion time after time.

You don't get it? No? But do hold on to your horses. Here let me get up and demonstrate. You can see the connected shape of the arms and torso right here as I rotate around my spine. Now watch how the hips rotate and transport the hands along with the torso. The hands come in slightly *higher* and a little more from the *inside* but exactly in the same fashion *time after time*. It's then a simple matter of tilting the machine and letting it re-peat its motion, like this, right here. Back and forth and back and forth like this. Isn't this a simple machine making a simple motion? Ah, your eyes widen and the jaw drops. Didn't I tell you that it's in plain view all the time, that it's so much in the face?

This little experiment here also gives us another im-portant insight into the Master's swing. The right arm always moves in sync with the rotation of the body and there is no arm-lift whatsoever by the left arm in any part of the Master's swing. The elevation of the hands for a brief instant at the top is solely the result of right-arm fold at the elbow.

By corollary therefore, there is no independent downward motion of the hands in his post-Secret swing. This is the reason why you will find no mention of a downswing in the Master's vocabulary. Instead, the Master chose to use the more appropriate term, the forward swing. He went with the term backswing, however, because it was appropriate and did not connote any upward motion. The Master's careful choice of words was a broad hint at the Secret. Did you think twice when you encountered the term forward swing? Did you wonder why he did not use the prevalent term downswing instead? No? It's okay; neither did the rest of us.

It consumed the Master totally, the idea of the machine with the Perfect and Automatic swing. He mischievously baptized it as Henny Bogan. From that time onwards the Master spent all his available waking hours looking for a way to actualize Henny Bogan. Along with the excitement came the doubt. The new embryonic swing was completely different from the one already ingrained deeply into his mind and body. Questions darted through his mind. How to do the backswing? How about the forward swing? How does one generate and maximize power? What about ball position? What about clubface orientation, trajectory and accuracy? But these issues did not daunt him. Neither did he let the lack of a college education deter him. He immersed himself in the study of basic physics, geometry and human bio-mechanics. He figured out everything in the end through sheer doggedness. The result was the Hogan Code. It is the key that enables the human golfer to mimic Henny Bogan. All the Master's fundamentals are directly derivable from the principles of Henny Bogan and are embodied in the Hogan Code.

In one fell swoop the three-dimensional degrees of freedom of the arm swing was reduced to a single degree of freedom of body rotation. Is it any wonder then that the Master who was not the most athletic or talented golfer of his times went on to become the greatest ball striker of all time?

The Master's fundamentals fall neatly in place like a jigsaw puzzle if the concept of the machine is understood.

May I request you for a repeat of the vodka martini? Yes, and some scrambled eggs too. No, not dinner.... just a snack to keep me going. All this talking has really made me hungry.

CHAPTER 4

Henny Bogan
Take Two

YOU REMEMBER THE ED Sullivan Show, the one
that half of America waited to watch on TV every Sun-
day? No, maybe you were much too young then to remember. The reason I mention it is because the Master
made an appearance on that show in 1951. He demonstrated his famous training exercise in that widely tele-
casted event.

"Clutch your sides with your elbows and visualize
your elbows attached to your body and arms instead of
the shoulders and just move your body from right to
left, around in a *circle*, holding your elbows in your
sides" the Master said and made a few short bidirectional swings. He then proceeded to lengthen the
motion with a series of complete and powerful swings

on either side and concluded: "Isn't that simple? Anyone can do that."

The Master was dead earnest. He could have repeated that movement *ad nauseam* and anybody else could have done it too, for that matter. There, right there, was the Secret in full view of the world. But people did not catch on to that one vital clue, did not put two and two together. What the Master demonstrated was a not-so-obvious feature of human anatomy. But the viewers of that episode took it for granted without further investigation at a conscious level.

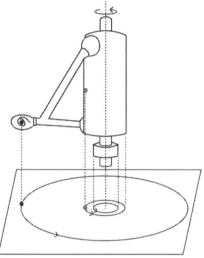

Henny Bogan Take Two. The shoulders, hips and right forearm behave like concentric cylinders when rotated around the central axis and generate three concentric circles on a horizontal plane.

In his book, the Master depicted the relative movements of the hips and shoulders using ellipses to represent cross-sections of the body at shoulder and hip levels. But he omitted to represent the actual concentric circular movement of the hips and shoulders. It is fairly obvious after all that both the hips and the shoulders rotate around the spinal axis.

Here, let me draw the circles. There are three circles, not two, please note. These are the very same three circles in the symbol of the Hogan Circle. I draw your attention to this third and large circle that the Master omitted. It is the circle of the hands and is defined by the extremity of the right forearm. The path of the right forearm projected on a horizontal plane is also circular and concentric with the circles of the shoulders and hips. So now we've put a finger on two of the Master's key omissions. The first is the *concentric circles* of the hips and shoulders. And the second is the addition of a *third circle*, the concentric circle of the hands.

In all golf swings, it is always the loaded right-forearm which paddlewheels into impact when it reaches the level of the hips. But the right forearm does not describe the circle of the arm swing. That is done by the left arm - the radius of the circle is the length of the left arm. The right forearm is loaded in the backswing from the level of the hips upwards by the elevating left arm in one of two ways. In a rotational swing the left arm elevates in sync with body turn. In a linear swing, the left arm elevates independent of body turn. The opposite happens in the forward swing. The right forearm passively paddlewheels into impact by the action of the left arm which moves either in sync with body turn as in the rotational swing or independently as in the linear swing.

The Master found out by study and through trial-and-error that the elevating action of the left arm could be suppressed and the right forearm could be made to describe the circle of the arm swing in complete *sync* with the body turn over a limited but definite range of motion. Here's what the Master discovered:

1) The connected shape of Henny Bogan is assembled in the backswing by a shoulder turn around the spinal axis while keeping the elbows as close as possible to the body. The hip turn is resisted by the right foot. The *level* shoulder rotation is made without any lateral slide. There is a small *resultant* lateral movement to the right as the joints of the right ankle, right knee and right hip stack up and the right leg straightens. But this is a *consequence* of the rotation and not a deliberate movement.

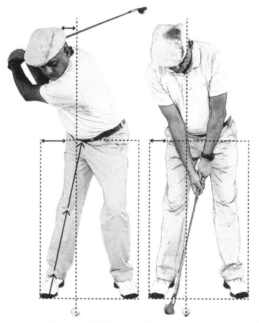

The connected shape of Henny Bogan is created by a level shoulder rotation around the spinal axis while keeping the elbows as close as possible to the body. The hip turn is resisted by the right foot. The stacking of joints in the right leg causes a small lateral movement to the right.

2) From a side-on posture in which the sternum faces the ball and the right elbow touches the right hipbone, the right forearm paddlewheels into impact as in a sidearm hitting or throwing motion. The right forearm motion is in a circular arc but its thrust is linear at an angle of 45 degrees.

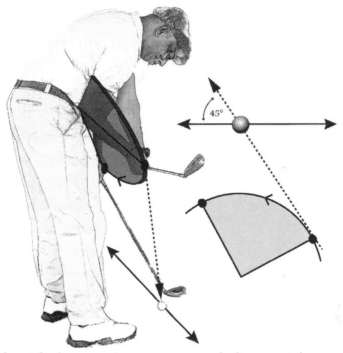

The right forearm thrusts in a straight line at 45 degrees as it paddlewheels into impact in a circular arc.

3) The shoulders can turn a maximum of 45 degrees around the spinal axis without lower-body movement. Further shoulder rotation is enabled only by riding on top of hip rotation. Hip rotation happens through the discrete stacking of joints of the right leg – the right ankle, right knee and right hip – on top of the right foot as the body weight shifts progressively to the right.

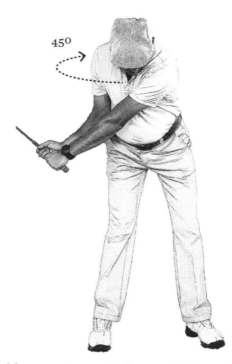

The shoulders can turn 45 degrees independent of movement in the lower body. Further shoulder rotation is enabled by hip rotation through the progressive stacking of the right ankle, right knee and right hip joints on top of the right foot.

4) Every stacked joint enables a hip rotation of 22.5 degrees and therefore an additional shoulder rotation of 22.5 degrees, or a quarter of a turn. The maximum possible backswing therefore has a shoulder rotation of 112.5 degrees or five quarter-turns. This is 45 degrees of independent shoulder rotation plus 67.5 degrees of hip-enabled rotation obtained by the stacking of the three lower-body joints. The hip rotation is fixed in both magnitude and direction and therefore yields predictable and repeatable motion of the shoulders.

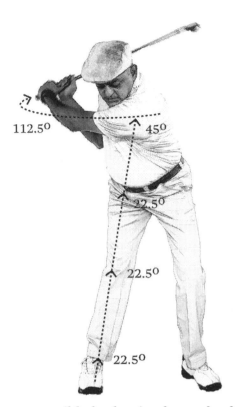

The maximum possible backswing has a shoulder rotation of five quarter-turns or 112.5 degrees which is 45 degrees of independent shoulder rotation plus 67.5 degrees of hip-enabled rotation.

5) *Flaring out* the left foot by 22.5 degrees - or a quarter of a turn - cuts back the hip rotation by 22.5 degrees. This is what the Master meant when he said that the feet are an excellent governor of hip turn. The maximum backswing is thus restricted to 90 degrees or four quarter-turns. This backswing has three stages of rotation. Two stages of 22.5 degrees each are obtained by hip rotation and one stage of 45 degrees is obtained through independent shoulder rotation.

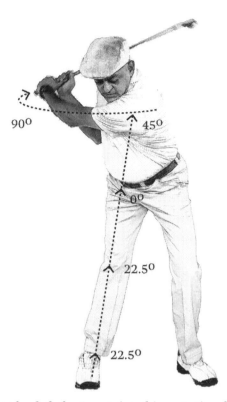

Flaring out the left foot restricts hip rotation by a quarter-turn or 22.5 degrees and results in a backswing of 90 degrees.

6) In a *top-down* backswing, the independent shoulder rotation happens first followed by the hip-enabled rotation. In a *bottom-up* backswing, the hip-enabled rotation happens first followed by the independent shoulder rotation. The left hip is turned first by leveraging the left foot against the ground. The right foot resists the left-hip turn; also by leveraging against the ground. This backswing gets automatic direction in the initial move away from the ball by the hip-enabled rotation.

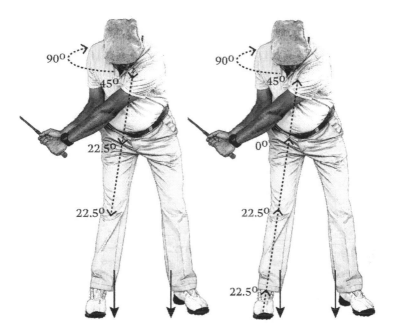

In the top-down backswing, the independent shoulder rotation happens first followed by the hip-enabled rotation. In the bottom-up backswing, the hip-enabled rotation happens first followed by independent shoulder rotation.

7) In the top-down backswing, the hips begin to rotate when the hands are at hip-level and the shoulders have turned 45 degrees. In the bottom-up backswing, the same position is attained when the hips have completed their rotation and the independent shoulder rotation is about to begin. But the sequence in the forward swing is the same: the hip-enabled rotation happens first and this time it is an unrestricted 67.5 degrees. The hip-rotation carries the hands to hip-level in the first 45 degrees and positions the right forearm in perfect trajectory to passively thrust at 45 degrees.

8) In either backswing, the right foot must resist the hip turn. This stacks the right hip-joint and sustains the circle of the right forearm. Without this, the right hip does not "clear", the hands elevate independently and the swing radius defaults to that of the left-arm circle.

9) The right hip joint stacks up when the hip rotation reaches its imit. When the shoulder rotation reaches its limit, the weight shifts to the left even as the right arm folds and the wrists hinge. The weight shift creates a dynamic and automatic transition.

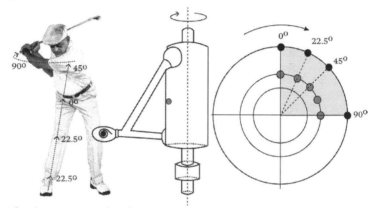

The bottom-up backswing is a rotation of 90 degrees with two stages of 22.5 degrees and a third stage of 45 degrees. This sequence is reversed in the top-down backswing.

10) The bottom-up backswing is a clockwise rotation from the ground up. The hips - and therefore the shoulders - wind up by 45 degrees as the joints of the right leg stack up. This winding-up of the shoulders has automatic direction since it is part of hip-enabled rotation. The last part of this backswing is the independent shoulder rotation of 45 degrees and it happens when the direction has already been irreversibly set.

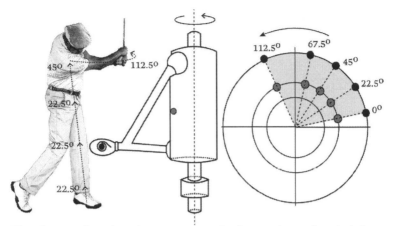

The forward swing is a symmetrical rotation of 112.5 degrees with three stages of 22.5 degrees each followed by a fourth stage of 45 degrees.

11) The forward swing is a counter-clockwise rotation from the ground up. The hips unwind by an unrestricted 67.5 degrees as the joints of the *left* leg stack up. The resultant unwinding of the shoulders has automatic direction since it is hip-enabled rotation. The last part of the forward swing is the independent shoulder rotation of 45 degrees and it happens when the direction has already been irreversibly set.

The Master did not completely detail what we have just discussed. But it is there all right, in his description of the lower body muscles to work with and his emphasis on the right foot flex. The most direct hint at the Secret is his insistence on the one and only correct stance: the right foot squared and the left foot flared out by 22 degrees. The principle of ground leverage in the Master's swing is the thought behind his famous and often-quoted remark: The Secret is in the Dirt. He knew that the obvious interpretation of his remark would be hard work, or the digging of dirt. It suited him just fine, given his love for the cryptic and the oblique. Does it make sense now? Good.

The principle of ground leverage is the thought behind the Master's famous quote: The Secret is in the Dirt.

The Master was overjoyed with his findings. He had discovered a method to automatically load and release the right forearm with body turn alone. He had the geometry all figured out. He next turned his attention to the physics – the application of power in the swing.

I think I'll have another vodka martini. You'll have another round as well? That's good. Have we already covered the Hogan Code, you ask? Well, we've covered some essential aspects of the Hogan Code but the big picture is yet to emerge. So please don't jump the gun. The time for your test is yet to come.

Enjoy the drink and relax for now. I can almost hear the wheels turning fast and hard inside your head.

CHAPTER 5

Henny Bogan
Take Three

YOU HAVE PLAYED BASEBALL? You even played for the college team? That's excellent. You were a privileged kid, though you may not think so. I wish sometimes I went to college, just to experience the camaraderie of playing a team sport. But again, I digress. Let me come back. Then you'll understand very well that we have used a baseball-like flat swing at the buckle level to arrive at Henny Bogan. But you've no doubt also understood that the only difference with respect to the golf swing is that Henny Bogan needs to be tilted in response to the ball placement on the ground. It's time now to discuss the specific tilt of Henny Bogan's motion and also the physics – the power aspect of the forward swing.

Here, let me sketch Henny Bogan Take Three for you. Its motion is driven by the rotation of the central axis. The arms act as passive clamps and are drawn around by rotation into impact and beyond. The right forearm moves in a circular arc in the closest possible proximity along the right side. The plane of this circle is perpendicular to the central axis. This is the Right Elbow Plane. It's the *undisclosed* and *dynamic* plane of the Master's swing.

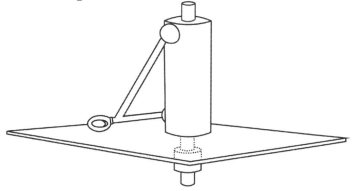

Henny Bogan Take Three. The circle of the right forearm lies on the Right Elbow Plane.

So then why did the Master depict his iconic pane of glass as resting on the shoulders, you ask? Well, the Master was right in his book with the pane of glass. But the *intent* behind it has been misinterpreted. If you attempt to make the shoulder turn under the pane of glass, you will be forced to turn level with the shoulders. The hands, arms and club head will not elevate independent of the body turn and thus cannot shatter the pane of glass. That was the Master's intent. He wasn't trying to show us the swing plane, which is by definition the two-dimensional plane created by the motion of the club shaft.

The Master was right with his iconic pane of glass as a visualization aid for making a level shoulder turn.

The actual plane of the Master's backswing is the Right Elbow Plane. At address, the *initial* and *static* state of this plane passes through the ball and the hips. The right elbow, the entire right forearm and the club shaft lie on this plane. This plane undergoes *continuous* and *dynamic* shift starting half-way into the backswing. At the top, the plane is shifted *up* and to the *right* compared to its initial orientation at address. These two distinct orientations of the dynamic Right Elbow Plane are respectively the initial planes of the Master's backswing and forward swing.

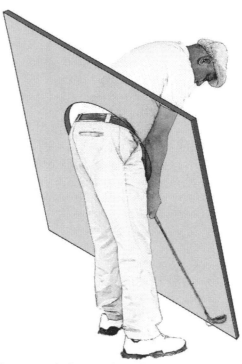

The initial state of the Right Elbow Plane is like a static pane of glass that passes through the hips and the ball.

The dynamic shifts of the Right Elbow Plane are complex but automatic and require no conscious thought or action. That's why the Master said that it's enough to know that the forward swing plane is shifted but that one must pay more attention to the backswing plane. The Master was really trying to make it simple for the reader to get the initial and static backswing plane right, you see? Once that's correct, the dynamic shifts are automatically taken care of by the rotation of the body. The Right Elbow Plane begins to shift halfway into the backswing and continues to shift three-fifths of the way into the forward swing.

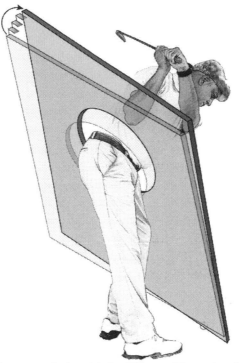

The initial state of the Right Elbow Plane in the forward swing is shifted up-and-right relative to its initial state in the backswing.

At this juncture, we must make a very important distinction between Henny Bogan the machine and Henny Bogan the golfer. In the machine, the axis of rotation remains stable. But in the golfer, the spinal axis of rotation moves continuously like that of a spinning top or gyroscope. This is because the golfer has one spinal axis and two legs while the machine has just the one central and common axis. The dynamic shifts of the Right Elbow Plane are a consequence of this gyroscopic motion of the spinal axis.

When examined with this perspective, this gyroscopic motion is readily observed in the Master's swing from one-half of the way in the backswing through to three-fifths of the way in the forward swing. The important thing to get is that both the spinal axis and the Right Elbow Plane move dynamically with body rotation. The head and tailbone are at opposite ends of the spinal axis and exhibit the same gyroscopic motion. Therefore a stationary head is *not* an attribute of the Master's swing.

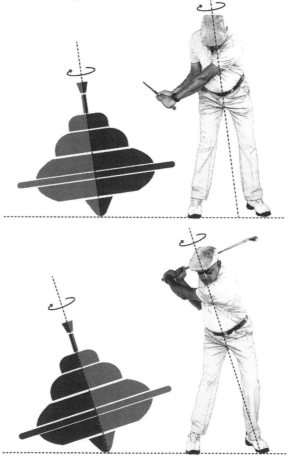

In Henny Bogan the golfer the spinal axis of rotation moves continuously similar to that of a spinning top.

Let's now discuss the application of power. The Master's method of applying power in the swing is counter-intuitive and accessible only through the Secret. The same stacking of joints in the lower body that creates the circular motion of Henny Bogan is also responsible for the creation of power or – to use the technically precise term - the generation of torque.

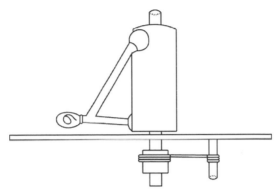

The complete Henny Bogan. The stacking of the three joints in the right leg obtained by leveraging the ground is like stretching the elastic band by three turns.

In the backswing, the joints of the right leg – the right ankle, right knee and right hip – stack up in a straight line. This is done by leveraging against the ground. The stacking of each joint is like stretching an elastic band by one turn. The stacking of three joints stretches the elastic band by three turns. We now add this elastic band to arrive at the complete Henny Bogan.

HENNY BOGAN IS DRIVEN BY ROTATION. THE BODY CAN ROTATE ONLY BECAUSE OF FRICTIONAL FORCES BETWEEN THE FEET AND GROUND. THE TORQUE IN HENNY BOGAN IS GENERATED BY LEVERAGING THE GROUND.

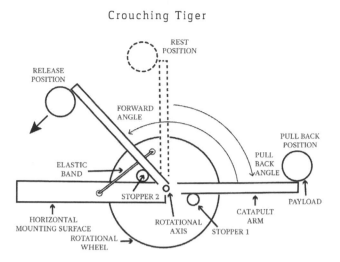

A top view of Henny Bogan resembles a Junior Science Catapult Kit.

A two-dimensional top view of Henny Bogan with the left arm omitted looks very similar to a Junior Science Catapult Kit illustrated above. The right forearm is the catapult arm; the left arm supports the right forearm as it rotates into impact. Does it come as any surprise that the Master often said that the role of the left arm is to support the right arm?

HENNY BOGAN IS A GOLFING CATAPULT THAT FIRES THE RIGHT FOREARM AND THE GOLF CLUB WITH LEVERAGED ROTATION.

In Henny Bogan, the backswing is analogous to the pull-back angle. The forward swing is analogous to the forward angle. The golf club is analogous to the payload. The hips are analogous to the rotational wheel. The stance of the feet that limits the backswing is analogous to the first stopper. The stalling of hip-rotation that causes the shoulders to go through is analogous to the second stopper. The stacking of the joints in the right leg is analogous to the elastic band. There is a difference in the plane of motion between the two machines. In the first, it is on a vertical plane while in the second, it is on an inclined plane. But both are catapult machines. The catapult principle has seen practical application at least three centuries before Christ. You've no doubt seen history feature films in which siege catapults were used to break down fortress walls?

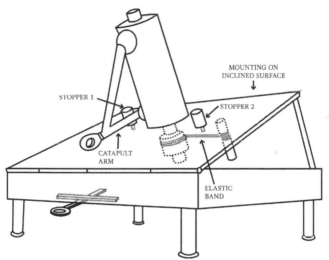

Henny Bogan the Body Swing Golfing Machine.

The *potential energy* created and stored in the elastic band during the backswing is converted into *kinetic energy* in the forward swing. This energy is first transmitted to the shoulders, then the arms, next to the hands and finally to the club head. The *rotational speed* is the same for all components but not the *linear speed*. The further the component is away from the axis of rotation, the greater is its linear speed. This is no rocket science; the outermost circle of horses in a carousel travels faster than the innermost one even though both go around in exactly the same time. The club head is the furthest and acquires a phenomenal linear speed by the time it reaches the ball. The club head can reach a linear speed upwards of hundred miles per hour when the torso has a linear speed of just a few miles per hour.

That's about it. We're done with the Resurrection of Henny Bogan. We've come to the very end, and it's time to put you to the test of the Sixth Lesson. What is the Hogan Code? Please proceed number by number, and state the significance of each one. Now what's the first?

Did you say 22.5 degrees? That the left foot is flared out by a quarter-turn at address? This is excellent work, my friend, excellent. You say that 22 degrees was an approximation the Master made in his book because higher precision would have invited further investigation? That's good thinking, my friend. You're beginning to get inside the Master's head. That's good, very good. We have the first number of the code, and it is 22.5 degrees indeed. Now how about the second?

Brilliant, my friend! It *is* zero degrees. You say that the squared position and stacking function of the right foot is absolutely critical in the Master's swing? Well done. The number zero isn't an obvious candidate after all. What's the third number?

Most obvious, do you say? Then what is it, may I ask? It is 90 degrees, indeed! The swing will not work without the full four-quarter turn of the shoulders in the backswing. Correct, it is two stages of hip-enabled rotation of 22.5 degrees each and one stage of 45 degrees of independent shoulder rotation. And yes, the actual sequence depends on whether it is a bottom-up or top-down backswing. You're doing well, very well. So what's the last and final number?

Did you say 112.5 degrees? Five quarter-turns, that's right. The forward swing is 112.5 degrees with three stages of hip-enabled rotation of 22.5 degrees each and a final stage of independent shoulder rotation of 45 degrees. You've nailed it!

Well done, my friend! The Hogan Code is indeed 22.5-0-90-112.5. The value of X is 22.5 degrees and A, B, C and D equal 1, 0, 4 and 5 respectively. All that remains now is to summarize.

The Hogan Code is 22.5-0-90-112.5.

Henny Bogan is by design the most powerful, accurate and repeatable swing in golf. It is an emulation of a catapult machine with a golf club as the payload. The machine has two setup angles of 22.5 degrees and 0 degrees respectively. It has two movement angles of 90 degrees and 112.5 degrees. These movement angles are created dynamically by using the natural maximum angles of human anatomy. They do not need to be monitored during the actual swing. The two setup angles are created from a static position at address and therefore do not pose a challenge. But they need to be created with care because they are the keys to Henny Bogan's motion. You no doubt recall the Master's remark that setting up correctly is eighty percent of the job done?

You'll also now fully appreciate what the Master meant when he said that he did not believe there was anything like a natural golf swing. Read between the lines and you understand that he meant *his* golf swing was a developed one. And what a development it was - the Master took 23 years to arrive at Henny Bogan. That was because he had no charted path to follow. But you, my friend, *now* have this knowledge, and that was the purpose of it all.

You've all that you need to write the book. This is all that's required to build the foundation of a golf game: a powerful and repeatable swing. It's a strong one, the very best possible, but it's still only the foundation. From information we've distilled knowledge. From knowledge you must distill wisdom. This can only be done by practice and experience. You'll need to build upon the foundation in all three dimensions – physical, mental and spiritual – before you can actualize yourself as a *golfer*. There is infinite potential in all three dimensions. This isn't rocket science either, just an attribute of being human. You'll discover that the greatest satisfaction is to be had from realizing this potential.

You, my friend, have the honor of being the last Hoganite by *selection*. Once the book is published, it'll supersede the Hogan Circle as custodian of the Master's Secret and vehicle of the Sixth Lesson. Anyone who'll discover, understand and apply the Master's techniques in the quest of perfection will become a Hoganite by *action*. The Hogan Circle will be dissolved on this completion of the Master's unfinished agenda. There wouldn't be any further need for it. It's with mixed feelings that I'll wait for that day.

I know that you'll do a good job; but let me state that your mandate is *not* to repeat what the Master has already said, but rather to help the golfer-reader understand and apply what he *meant*. This is my vision for what the book must achieve for the golfer-reader:

CROUCHING TIGER IS IN YOU. HIDDEN HOGAN IS ALSO IN YOU. BOTH THE POTENTIAL AND THE ABILITY TO UNLEASH IT IS WITHIN YOU. GO FORTH AND PLAY THE GAME THE WAY IT WAS MEANT TO BE PLAYED: AT GOD'S FEET.

And so, my friend, the time's come to say farewell for now. Here's my visiting card. Come and see me when you're done.

Epilogue

IT WAS WITH EXCITEMENT and anxiety that I stepped out of the Shinkansen bullet train at Yashikima Prefecture. I ran my fingertips over the dust jacket of the hardbound book. I hoped Kojiro would approve.

It was a large and traditional Japanese house with a garden of azalea and maple trees. There was a miniature cascade with a koi fishpond at its bottom. The kimono-clad lady who opened the door was serene and stately.

"But there's no Hiroki Kojiro here," she said. The smile was benign, the English impeccable.

"Excuse me, ma'am, but this is the address he gave me." I fumbled in my pocket and handed over the visiting card.

"I'm sorry, sir, but I'm afraid there's a mistake. This is the ancestral Isutani home. Our family has lived here for generations."

I hung my head, mumbled an apology and started to turn around. I saw it out of the corner of my eye, the large frame in the wall above the shoe rack in the entrance area. It depicted an industrial Henny Bogan, but with a transparent and retracted plane. The body had a steel brushed finish and the chassis looked like sheet metal. I could discern through the transparent plane that the elastic band had been replaced by a torsion spring. But there was no mistaking the resemblance to the makeshift sketches that Kojiro had done for me.

クラウチング・タイガー　ヒデン・ホーゴーン

"Please excuse me, ma'am." I craned my neck and peered at the boilerplate inscription bolted into the chassis.

Speed Testing Machine
The Ben Hogan Golf Company
2912 West Pafford Street
Fort Worth, Texas, USA
2250901125

A shudder ran down my spine. It all started to make sense. It made perfect sense. It was all up to the book now.

Book Two:
Crouching Tiger

CHAPTER 1

Fundamentals

AS PER KOJIRO'S MANDATE the focus is not on re-peating what the Master has already said, but on filling the gaps in understanding and execution. Henny Bogan must be understood by starting off with the *fundamentals*. The Master's fundamentals are those principles of Henny Bogan that cannot be changed without compromising its motion.

THE FUNDAMENTALS ARE THE SETUP AND MOVE-MENT PRINCIPLES OF HENNY BOGAN. THE SETUP FUNDAMENTALS ARE GRIP, ADDRESS AND WAGGLE. THE MOVEMENT FUNDAMENTALS ARE BACKSWING AND FORWARD SWING.

Henny Bogan must be positioned, set up and operated correctly to yield the desired result. First, one must fit the tool into Henny Bogan's chuck correctly. This is the grip fundamental. Second, Henny Bogan must be positioned correctly. This is the address fundamental.

Third, there must be a way of checking Henny Bogan's placement and tool fitment. This is the waggle fundamental. Fourth, Henny Bogan must be loaded correctly. This is the backswing fundamental. Fifth, Henny Bogan must be fired correctly. This is the forward swing fundamental. Finally, there must be a way to monitor Henny Bogan. This is the sixth fundamental.

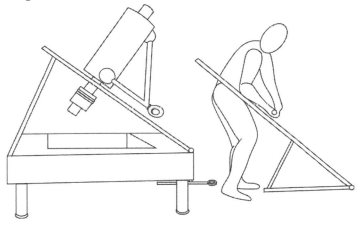

The Master's fundamentals can be derived directly from the setup and movement principles of Henny Bogan.

Henny Bogan's swing is a body-driven circular motion and all the fundamentals relate to the creation and sustenance of the circle of the hands – located at the extremity of the right forearm - on the dynamic Right Elbow Planc.

The Grip

In Henny Bogan, the hands function as a chuck to hold a tool called the golf club. The chuck moves on the Right Elbow Plane. The wrists function as a door hinge joint. The correct grip allows the wrists to bend together as one unit.

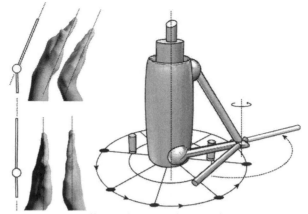

The correct grip allows both palms to hinge and unhinge around the wrists on an axis perpendicular to the Right Elbow Plane.

THE GRIP FUNDAMENTAL: HENNY BOGAN'S CHUCK FUNCTIONS LIKE A DOOR HINGE WITH THE CORRECT GRIP.

The hinging and unhinging action of the chuck is on an axis *perpendicular* to the Right Elbow Plane. A neutral grip has both the palms squarely facing each other and allows both wrists to bend together and remain perpendicular to the plane. A strong grip turns the left palm relative to the right palm and positions it off-plane. This is the reason why weakening his grip was one of the changes the Master had to make to implement the Secret.

The Address

The left foot is flared out by 22.5 degrees and the right foot is squared to the target line. As we have seen, the orientation of the feet is crucial in Henny Bogan. This orientation also puts the flared left foot in perfect position to torque and the squared right foot to resist.

The target line should be a tangent to the arc for every club in the bag. This is an in-to-square-to-in circular arc.

Henny Bogan's placement on the ground needs to be adjusted to accommodate different club lengths. The reason, of course, is that the arcs get longer with the longer clubs and shorter with shorter clubs. There will be just one club that will fit Henny Bogan's motion without any alteration in a squared shoulder line and a squared stance line. This club will have an in-to-square-to-in arc of the takeaway. In other words, the target line will be a *tangent* to the takeaway. Any club longer than this one will have an out-to-in takeaway arc with an unaltered address. Any club shorter than this will have an in-to-out takeaway arc with an unaltered address.

The club length can be accommodated by changing one of two variables while keeping the other constant: ball position or right foot position. The Master's guiding principle in making this choice was that Henny Bogan must have the same *feel* irrespective of the tool mounted on the chuck.

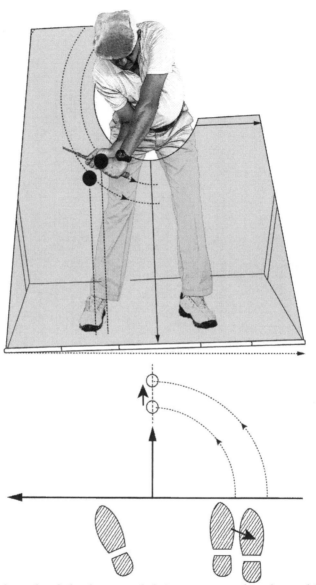

The length of the longer club is accommodated at address by moving the right foot down and to the right. For all club lengths, the release arc in the forward swing always begins when the hands reach hip level and are above and in front of the right foot.

Changing the ball position is a viable option but it changes the visual *feel* of Henny Bogan as the golfer addresses the ball with clubs of different lengths. But changing the right foot position retains the same visual feel because the ball position *feels* constant for all club lengths and was therefore the Master's chosen option.

Withdrawing the right foot away from the target line moves the takeaway arc inside while advancing it towards the target line moves the arc outside. Finding the correct right foot position to get the desired takeaway arc for the selected club is part of the address routine. The right foot must be positioned for every club such that the target line is a tangent to the takeaway arc. When done correctly, the angle between every pair of ball position and corresponding right foot position is automatically set to 45 degrees. The adjustment of the right foot position must be done without changing the orientation of the feet: the left foot is still flared out by 22.5 degrees and the right foot is still square to the target line.

THE ADDRESS FUNDAMENTAL: HENNY BOGAN IS POSITIONED ON THE GROUND BY FLARING OUT THE LEFT FOOT BY 22.5 DEGREES AND SQUARING THE RIGHT FOOT.

Changing the right foot position by advancing or withdrawing it from the target line was the Master's preferred way to accommodate the arc of the selected club. However it is not a fundamental. Varying the ball position is also a viable option and may be chosen as a personal modification.

The Waggle

The waggle is used to verify Henny Bogan's placement and tool fitment. The wrists start to unhinge in the forward swing when (a) the club shaft is parallel to the ground, (b) the hands are at hip level and (c) the right forearm touches the right hipbone at the right elbow. The waggle is a replay of this release action.

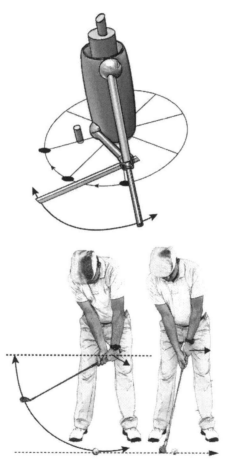

The waggle is a replay of the release action of the wrists in the forward swing. The target line is a tangent to the takeaway and return arcs of the waggle.

The waggle is done by bending the right wrist which in turn bends the left wrist and causes the right elbow to touch the right hipbone. With full right-wrist bend the club shaft should be on-plane and aligned parallel to the ground. A strong grip cannot do this. The takeaway and approach arcs of the club head created by the waggle have a tangential relationship with the target line. The waggle verifies the on-plane radial distance of the right forearm from the ball for the selected club.

THE WAGGLE FUNDAMENTAL: HENNY BOGAN'S PLACEMENT AND TOOL FITMENT IS CHECKED BY THE WAGGLE. IT VERIFIES THE ON-PLANE RADIAL DISTANCE OF THE RIGHT FOREARM FROM THE BALL FOR THE SELECTED CLUB.

The Backswing

The purpose of the backswing is to assemble and load Henny Bogan. Henny Bogan begins to assemble 45 degrees into the backswing. In the bottom-up backswing, the elastic band begins to stretch immediately and attains full stretch when the shoulders have rotated 45 degrees. In the top-down backswing, the elastic band begins to stretch after 45 degrees of shoulder rotation and attains full stretch when the shoulders have rotated 90 degrees. The *limit* of shoulder rotation simultaneously concludes the backswing, triggers the weight shift and completes the dynamic transition.

THE BACKSWING FUNDAMENTAL: HENNY BOGAN IS ASSEMBLED AND LOADED BY A 90 DEGREE CIRCULAR ARC OF THE HANDS ON THE DYNAMIC RIGHT ELBOW PLANE.

Henny Bogan is assembled and loaded in the backswing by a 90 degree circular path of the hands. The connected shape is assembled 45 degrees into the backswing.

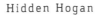

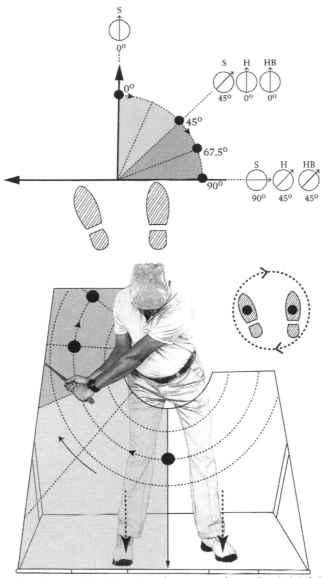

The circular path of the hands mapped on the initial Right Elbow Plane of the backswing. The plane undergoes continuous and dynamic shift after the shoulders have turned 45 degrees. The sequence illustrated here is the top-down backswing. S=Shoulders, H=Hips, HB=Henny Bogan.

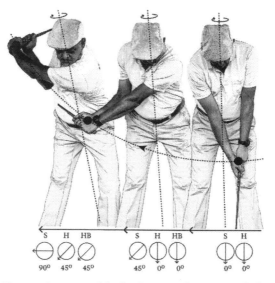

Henny Bogan is assembled after 45 degrees of shoulder rotation. The sequence illustrated here is the top-down backswing. S=Shoulders, H=Hips, HB=Henny Bogan.

The Forward Swing

The purpose of the forward swing is to fire Henny Bogan. Its rotation in the opposite direction releases the fully-stretched elastic band. The forward swing consists of three lower-body stages of 22.5 degrees each followed by one upper-body stage of 45 degrees. These stages *appear* as a rotation around the left side as the joints of the left leg stack up. The hips stall after 67.5 degrees and cause the shoulders to go through in the last 45 degrees. The forward swing happens as one uninterrupted chain reaction.

THE FORWARD SWING FUNDAMENTAL: HENNY BOGAN IS FIRED THROUGH A 112.5 DEGREE CIRCULAR ARC OF THE HANDS ON THE DYNAMIC RIGHT ELBOW PLANE.

Henny Bogan is fired in the forward swing by a 112.5 degree circular path of the hands. Lower body acceleration happens in the first 67.5 degrees. Impact and extension happen in the last 45 degrees.

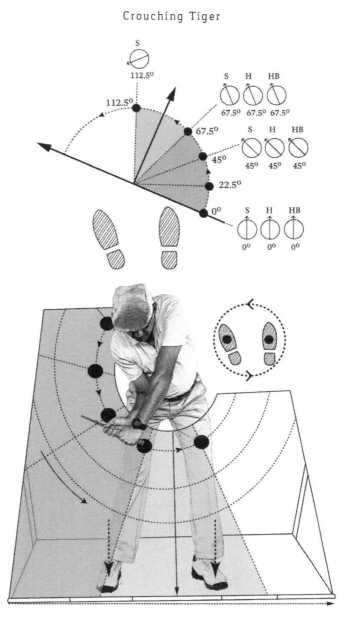

The circular path of the hands mapped on the initial Right Elbow Plane of the forward swing. The plane undergoes continuous and dynamic shift in the first 67.5 degrees. Henny Bogan is fired when the hips stall and the shoulders go through. S=Shoulders, H=Hips, HB=Henny Bogan.

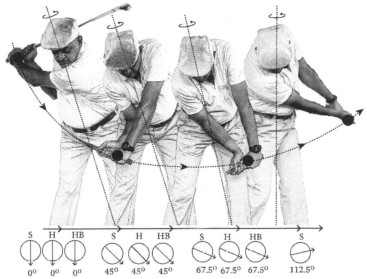

Henny Bogan is intact 67.5 degrees into the forward swing.
S=Shoulders, H=Hips, HB=Henny Bogan.

The Sixth Fundamental

The hips play a pivotal role in Henny Bogan. The ground forces due to hip rotation are felt as pressure points in the feet. These points move up and down each foot as the rotation starts, changes direction and progresses the other way. A vertical pane of glass resting against the hips rotates like an opening and closing door. The *weight distribution line* drawn through corresponding pair of pressure points in the feet is always parallel to the rotating pane of glass. This enables the monitoring of the swing movement with the feet.

THE SIXTH FUNDAMENTAL: HENNY BOGAN IS EXECUTED BY MONITORING THE PIVOT - THE FEET, HIPS AND SHOULDERS.

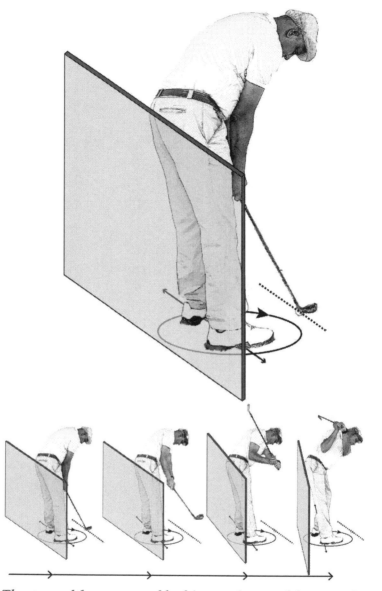

The ground forces caused by hip rotation are felt as moving pressure points in the soles of the feet. This aspect of Henny Bogan enables the monitoring of the swing movement with the feet.

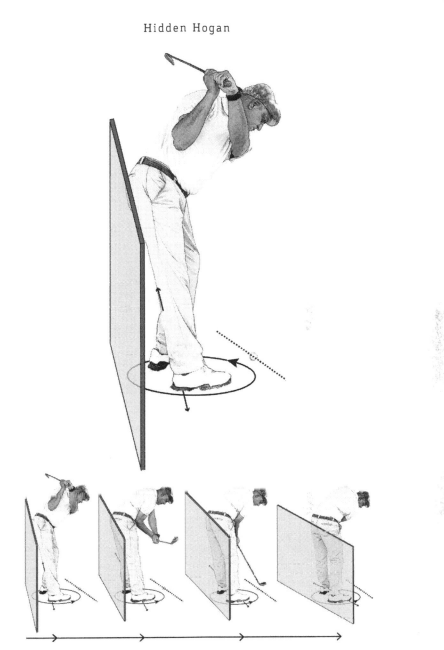

The weight distribution line drawn through corresponding pair of pressure points in the feet is always parallel to a vertical pane of glass that rests against and rotates with the hips.

The anatomical angles of 22.5 degrees per joint for lower-body enabled rotation and 45 degrees for independent shoulder turn are the normal averages. Hence for most golfers the backswing arc will be 90 degrees and the forward swing arc will be 112.5 degrees.

However, some golfers may have proportionately less or more range of motion - values of X specific to individuals and different from the 22.5 degrees number used in this book. The symmetry of the Hogan Code still applies for different values of X:

AX-BX-CX-DX

A, B, C and D will still have values of 1, 0, 4 and 5 respectively. For an individual with less-than-average flexibility, X may have a value of 22 degrees. The Hogan Code for this individual is 22-0-88-110. For another individual with more-than-average flexibility, X may have a value of 23 degrees. The Hogan Code for this individual is 23-0-92-115. Henny Bogan will work nonetheless for both individuals provided that the shoulder turn is stretched to the individual's pre-programmed limit.

CHAPTER 2

Implementation

HENNY BOGAN IS CONTAINED within the anatomy of every reasonably coordinated golfer. But the golfer's existing setup and movement is certain to be different from Henny Bogan's. Furthermore all golfers may not have the ability to execute the Master's implementation of Henny Bogan. Therefore *personal modifications* are needed to adapt the individual's Henny Bogan as per ability and other considerations. A set of personal modifications is an *implementation* that unlocks the golfer's Henny Bogan *without* compromising the fundamentals. The truly blessed golfer is one who has to make the *least* number of personal modifications.

There are personal modifications possible in grip, stance, address and backswing but *not* in the forward swing because that is an absolute.

The Grip: Types and Strength

The Master discovered through trial and error that the Vardon grip worked best for him. However, one may choose from the four different types: Vardon, Reverse Overlap, Interlocking and the Baseball grip. The *type* of grip a golfer adapts is a personal modification and not a fundamental.

However the *relative* orientation of the hands in regard to each other is a fundamental. Both palms must face each other to enable the proper hinging action of *both* wrists on an axis *perpendicular* to the Right Elbow Plane. The acid test of the correct grip is the on-plane, full wrist bend of both hands. This is tested by the waggle. On-plane and full wrist bend of both hands cannot be achieved by a strong grip.

The Stock Shot: Draw and Fade

Subject to the mandatory requirement of full wrist bend, the strength of the left hand in the grip is a personal modification within limits. The left hand may be turned in the grip to achieve the desired ball flight of the stock shot.

In golf we need a stock shot, a go-to shot that will give us a predictable and repetitive ball flight. This is the practiced-and-rehearsed staple shot that a golfer will play time and again unless exceptional circumstances such as wind or obstructions demand a specialty shot: draw, fade, high or low as the case maybe. Ball flight is a result of swing path and club face orientation. Changing the swing path is not an option with Henny Bogan but the clubface orientation can be modified in the grip to yield the ball flight of the stock shot. With a neutral grip, the default ball flight is a slight draw. Other desired ball-flight shapes are obtained by changing the clubface orientation accompanied by an adjustment in the stance line. It was a simple thing for the Master to obtain a power fade by opening the stance and further weakening his grip so that the clubface was slightly open at impact.

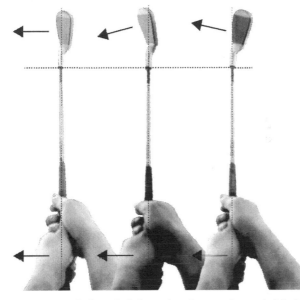

The orientation of the clubface is changed to yield the desired ball flight of the stock shot along with corresponding adjustment in the stance line.

The Address: Right Foot and Ball Positions

It is possible to address the issue of differing club lengths in one of two ways. The variables are ball position and right foot position. One of them may be varied while keeping the other constant. The Master chose to alter the right foot position rather than the ball position because he did not want to change the visual *feel* of

Henny Bogan's placement and motion for different club lengths. But changing the ball position is a viable option and may be chosen as a personal modification. Altering the right foot position moves the arc *down* and *right* while altering the ball position moves the arc *up* and *left*. Both achieve the same goal of accommodating the wider arc of the longer club.

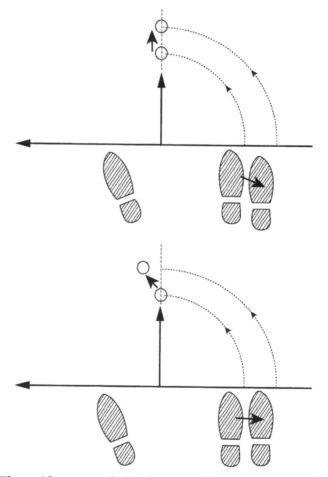

The wider arc of the longer club is accommodated by changing either the right foot position or the ball position.

The Backswing

The top-down backswing is already well chronicled and widely understood. The bottom-up backswing is described here as a personal modification.

The bottom-up backswing is a simultaneous rotation of the *left* hip and *right* shoulder from the *ground up*. The left hip is turned by leveraging the left foot against the ground. The right foot resists by leveraging against the ground. The backswing is done while *attempting* to keep the arms down. Any conscious arm-lift disrupts the arm-body sync and results in an error. The right shoulder must be turned such that the arc of the club head is on the *circle of the right forearm*. This is smaller, tighter and shallower than the circle of the left arm. This tight shoulder turn with the elbows close to the sides feels very much like turning in a barrel.

The right hip-joint stacks up after the hips (and shoulders) have rotated 45 degrees and the hands are at the level of the hips. The shoulders now begin their independent rotation. The right elbow folds and the wrists hinge. The weight shifts as the tailbone turns and points down at the left foot and the body seeks to preserve its balance. The right shoulder should be turned to the limit in order to trigger the dynamic transition. The guarantee against over-swinging is not in the shoulder turn itself, but in the pre-programmed limit built into the stance and *sustained* by the resistance of the squared right foot. This limit is reached at the top when the left shoulder comes under the chin. The dynamic transition is already complete at this point. The *feel* checkpoints at the top are (a) left shoulder under chin and (b) weight shift to the left foot.

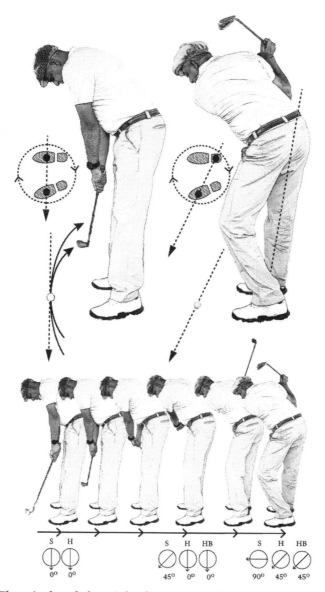

The circle of the right forearm is shorter and tighter than the circle of the left arm. The sequence illustrated here is the top-down backswing. S=Shoulders, H=Hips, HB=Henny Bogan.

The simultaneous left hip-right shoulder rotation creates a *bidirectional* swing where the backswing and forward swing feel similar. Strictly speaking, they are not because the trigger, rotational speed and plane of the forward swing are different from those of the backswing. But bi-directionality makes the swing fluid and free-flowing. The left hip leads the right shoulder *both ways* in the bidirectional swing. It should feel as if the left hip is turning the right shoulder away in the backswing and the left hip is returning the right shoulder back in the forward swing. It is difficult not to start the forward swing with the left hip when the backswing has been initiated by it in the first place.

The Forward Swing

The forward swing is an absolute. It is regardless of any personal modifications in grip, stance, address and backswing. The forward swing is powered by a chain reaction using the body's natural kinematic sequence.

The golfer becomes aware of the power at the top when the weight shifts to the left foot. The golfer senses the tremendous leverage available to whip around Henny Bogan with the hips. The forward swing is *triggered* with an aggressive turn of the left hip by leveraging the left foot against the ground. The left hip is turned even as the club is still going back but the arms have reached their limit.

It is the lower body that moves while the upper body, including the hands and arms, simply go for the ride. It will feel as if the hips are carrying the hands forward and all the way around. Actually the hips carry the hands to right above the ball before they stall.

The forward swing is driven by the lower body. The upper body including the hands and arms simply go for the ride. Henny Bogan fires when the hips stall and the right shoulder goes through. S=Shoulders, H=Hips, HB=Henny Bogan.

After the hips stall, it is the shoulders that carry the hands forward in the same uninterrupted motion. Impact and extension happen naturally during this last phase of shoulder rotation.

The chain reaction is triggered by the left hip. But before the left hip joint can stack up, the left ankle-joint and the left knee-joint have to necessarily stack up first. The body executes this stacking sequence naturally. The shoulders ride on top of all the lower-body joints and rotate as a consequence.

The power is generated by the ground-leveraged pivot: the big muscles of the left leg, left thigh and lower left back *but not the left shoulder*. The left shoulder is completely passive throughout the swing. It is the *right shoulder* that fires passively when the hips run out of rotation. The shoulders cannot trigger the chain reaction because the number of the right shoulder is *fourth* in the sequence after the left ankle, the left knee and the left hip. This timing and power sequencing is built into Henny Bogan. It uses the power of both sides of the body. The only way to increase this power is to turn harder against the ground. Hand-and-arm action sabotages the chain reaction and results in misfiring Henny Bogan.

The left hip right shoulder combination is *not interchangeable* with the right hip-left shoulder combination. In Henny Bogan, there is a crisscross partnership between lower-body stacks and shoulders. The *active* and *torqueing* stack in both backswing and forward swing is the left lower-body stack and its partner is the right shoulder. The *passive* and *resisting* stack is the right lower-body stack and its partner is the left shoulder.

Implementations of Henny Bogan

Implementations are based on personal modifications in grip, stock shot, stance, address and backswing. Three examples are illustrated: the Master's implementation, an easy one and an unorthodox one.

The Master's Implementation

The Master's implementation was chosen subject to three considerations. First, get a power fade as the desired ball flight of the stock shot. Second, keep the changes to a minimum. Third, hide the Secret.
- Weak Grip
- Variable Right Foot Position
- Top-Down Backswing
- Big Lateral Motion both ways

An Easy Implementation

An easy implementation is based on the following considerations. First, get a slight draw as the desired ball flight for the stock shot. Second, make the least number of personal modifications to existing setup. Third, have the simplest and most repeatable motion.
- Neutral Grip
- Variable Ball Position
- Top-Down Backswing
- Small Lateral Motion both ways

The small lateral motion on either side is not a *deliberate* movement. Rather it is a consequence of rotation and stacking of joints in the right and left legs in the backswing and forward swings respectively.

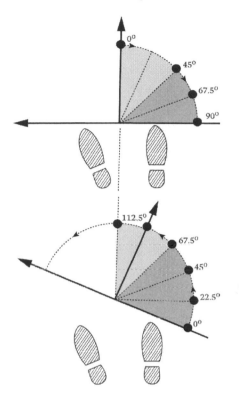

The Master's implementation is a dual-plane one with distinct planes for backswing and forward swing.

An Unorthodox Implementation

All orthodox implementations have distinct planes for backswing and forward swing. The plane of the forward swing can be distinctly *felt* as shifting *up* and to the *right* as the tailbone rotates towards the left foot and the weight shifts during transition.

An unorthodox but effective implementation is where one starts off at address with the weight set on the *left* foot and the joints of the *left* leg stacked. This causes the shoulder line to shift *rightwards* and *upwards*. The ball position is fixed in the center of the stance line, but is actually forward with respect to the shifted shoulder line. There will be a gap between the ball and the natural rest position of the club which is at the center of the shoulder line. This gap will increase with longer clubs. The weight is to the left at address but moves to the right in the backswing and shifts back to the left during transition.

- Neutral Grip
- Fixed Ball Position
- Bottom-Up Backswing
- No Lateral Motion either way

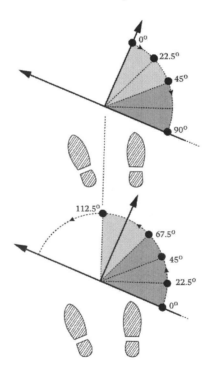

A single-plane implementation with leftwards weight at address and shoulder line shifted to forward swing plane.

The Master's implementation is not the *recommended* one because the big lateral motions on both sides are neither *useful* nor *easy* to do. The Master made a *conscious* decision to stop short of actualizing the Perfect and Automatic swing in its rotational entirety. He retained the big lateral motion of his old swing even though it had become redundant after his discovery of Henny Bogan. His consideration was to retain his competitive advantage by hiding Henny Bogan from the vigilant eyes of his more athletic and talented rivals on the Tour. It was a brilliant trade-off: the final cut from the Master of Camouflage.

The Master's lateral motion to the right serves to conceal the assembly of Henny Bogan in the backswing by moving the right elbow away from the right side. Henny Bogan becomes visible in the Master's swing only at the top when the Master makes another lateral motion to the left that *compensates* for the first lateral motion to the right *and* connects the right elbow to the right side. These lateral motions on both sides do not contribute to either accuracy or power, but they served very well the Master's purpose of hiding Henny Bogan.

So, then, maybe, the right question to ask is why would you choose to do as the Master did if your considerations are not the same as his?

CHAPTER 3

Execution

ONCE THE SUITABLE IMPLEMENTATION has been chosen, it is a simple thing to execute Henny Bogan. The bottom-up backswing is used here instead of the familiar top-down backswing to illustrate execution. The difference, as we have seen, is that the hips lead in the former while the shoulders lead in the latter.

Henny Bogan is 80% setup and 20% movement. Of the 20% movement, the first 10% is the first move away from the ball and the second 10% is the first move from the top. These are what the Master called the two crossroads in the swing.

The left hip-right shoulder takeaway is done by leveraging the left-hip turn with the left foot and resisting it with the right. The tension in the right leg is maintained. The left shoulder under the chin is anticipated. The left hip is then turned hard against the ground.

Everything else happens naturally and on its own.

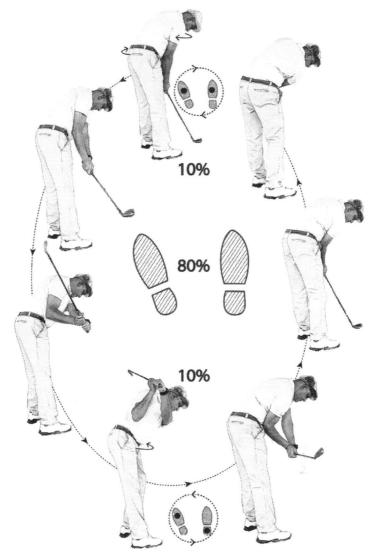

10%

80%

10%

The left hip-right shoulder takeaway from the ball is done by leveraging the left-hip turn with the left foot and resisting it with the right. The tension in the right leg is maintained. The left shoulder under the chin is anticipated. The left hip is then turned hard against the ground.

Hoganisms

THE MASTER WAS ADEPT not just at golf. He was a past master at camouflage too. The Master chose to play the Pied Piper in his book. He did not give away the Secret outright but placed ingenious clues throughout the book. Outside of it, he made famously quoted statements that were cryptic or had a double meaning or were contradictions in terms. I like to use the word *Hoganism* to represent these clues and decoys. Here we examine Hoganisms and try to demystify them. We also look at some other aspects of the Master's swing.

Three Right Hands

The most controversial Hoganism is the Master's wish for three right hands. Why did he not also wish for three left hands, especially after he stated that you must hit as hard with the left as with the right? The answer lies in simple physics. In Henny Bogan, the hands move in a circular arc centered on the spinal axis with radius equal to the length of the right forearm plus the distance of the right elbow from the spine. However for simplicity we shall disregard the small distance from right elbow to the spine.

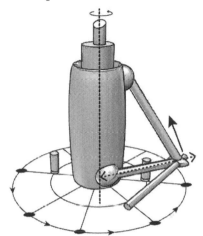

All components of Henny Bogan have the same angular speed but the linear speed of the hands is the common angular speed multiplied by the length of right forearm.

In Henny Bogan, the left arm and right forearm are passive and serve as clamps that transmit the power of the rotating hips and shoulders to the hands. Henny Bogan rotates as one unit and all its components have the same *rotational* speed at any point of time. But the *linear* speed of any component is proportional to its radial distance from the axis of rotation.

What the Master really wished for was a right forearm that was three times *longer*. That would have tripled the length of the right forearm and tripled the speed of the hands. But the Master could not have explicitly said so without giving away the Secret. So the Master said three right hands and left it as a cryptic clue for readers to figure it out. Most readers inferred that the Master was hitting with his right hand and wished for three right arms to hit the ball harder. That cannot be correct because there is no place for independent arm thrust in Henny Bogan. It is rotational force − torque - all the way from start to finish.

This is the correct interpretation of the controversial Three Right Hands statement made by the Master.

One may want to do a simple experiment to verify the Three Right Hands observation. Take any door in your house. This is a vertical plane hinged to the side of the doorframe. The base of the door moves over the floor which is a horizontal plane. The base of the door represents the right forearm and the floor represents the Right Elbow Plane. With the door half open, place a golf ball close to the hinged edge of the door and another ball close to the free end of the door. The distance of the second ball from the hinged end should be three times the distance of the first ball from the hinged end. Now open the door fully by withdrawing it towards the wall. This is the backswing away from both balls. Next pull the door shut with some force. This is the forward swing through both balls. As the door slams shut, it will go through both balls in its rotational path. The ball that was closer to the outside edge will take off exactly three times faster and travel three times further than the other ball. This is no rocket science. It is the same principle that yields longer distances with clubs of longer lengths.

Supination and Pronation

One of the most notable aspects of the Master's swing is the retention of lag deep into the forward swing.

The Master's design of Henny Bogan required that the clubface be square to the arc throughout the swing. This can be done by hinging the wrists early as in the waggle and then freezing them in that squared position for the rest of the swing. But there is a catch – the release action then has to be a hitting or throwing action with the right forearm. But the Master wanted the release action to be caused by body rotation and not by arm or hand action. The Master was stumped temporarily before he discovered something that happens quite naturally in the golf swing: forearm rotation.

In the backswing the right forearm rotates clockwise by 90 degrees. This is called pronation. Pronation is reversed in the forward swing as the right forearm rotates counterclockwise by 90 degrees. This is called supination. Pronation opens up the square clubface of the takeaway arc. Supination squares up the open clubface of the approach arc. All this may seem trivial at first because the two simply cancel out each other. So why then did the Master go overboard with the much publicized Hoganism of supination and pronation?

The most efficient way to swing a golf club is to swing the handle, not the club head. Swinging the handle is applying *longitudinal* acceleration to the club head along the length of the club shaft. This is the most efficient way because it retains lag in the forward swing and causes a delayed release. The Master was overjoyed because pronation and supination gave him a natural and automatic way to retain his lag deep into the forward swing.

Longitudinal acceleration is built into Henny Bogan. The pronated right forearm allowed the Master to apply longitudinal pressure through hip-rotation starting from the top without having to artificially hold on to the wrist hinge by hand action. Pronation keeps the wrist hinge intact late into the forward swing till the hands reach the level of the hips. Supination starts to square up the clubface at the level of the hips when the wrists begin to unhinge and the impact interval begins. This is the most delayed release possible. The hands do not deliberately hold on to the wrist hinge. The wrists are passive and supple throughout the swing.

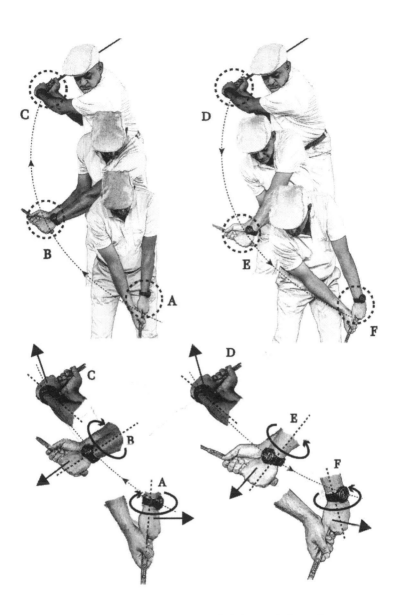

Pronation opens up the square clubface of the takeaway arc while supination squares up the open clubface of the approach arc.

The Free Ride of the Hands and Arms

This celebrated Hoganism which states that the hands and arms get a free ride when the hips initiate the forward swing was made in a limited context. The Master stopped short of saying something far more fundamental and important. In Henny Bogan, the arms are completely passive so that the reliance on arm-body timing is zero. The role of the arms is to passively transmit the torque generated by the rotating torso, first by hip rotation and then by shoulder rotation. The hands and wrists are passive throughout the forward swing. The release action is natural, passive and automatic. *The arms, hands and wrists get a free ride throughout the forward swing.*

The Secret in the Dirt

This Hoganism is possibly the most iconic one. The Master knew that it would be interpreted as the digging of dirt to unearth the treasure of the Secret. But that is not what he meant.

Henny Bogan is powered by rotation. The body can rotate only by leveraging against the ground. The torque is generated by shear forces between the feet and the ground. The torque can be increased only by maximizing these shear forces since the arm swing is passive.

The feedback from the shear forces is felt in the shifting pressure points in the feet. This feedback allows Henny Bogan's motion to be monitored by the feet.

In Henny Bogan, the secret to both power and movement is in the dirt.

In Henny Bogan the secret to both power and movement is in the dirt.

The Basketball Pass

It is possible to use the Master's geometry and still propel the golf swing with a hitting or throwing action of the right forearm preceded by an initial clearing action of the hips. In fact that is what most people have done in their attempts to emulate the Master's swing. The Master himself appears to have suggested a throwing action with the Hoganism of the two-handed basketball pass. A two-handed basketball pass is an *active* throwing out of the hands with the arms. The motion of Henny Bogan looks similar to the basketball pass, but the hands are thrown out *passively*. It is difficult to distinguish the body swing from the arm swing when the geometry is identical.

However, more often than not, it is the finish that is the giveaway. The body swing will almost always end in perfect, stacked and balanced finish. The arm swing will finish perfectly only when the arm-body timing is perfect. What the Master intended to communicate with the basketball pass example was the inside-square-inside trajectory of the passive arm swing. Why use Henny Bogan and revert to an arms-driven swing and regress to the arm-body timing paradigm? There are other geometries available for making an arms-driven swing. Henny Bogan's special geometry creates a passive and automatic arm-swing with the rotation of the body.

How the Master took out the Left Side of the Fairway

The Master disliked the right-to-left ball flight because it was the signature of the hook, his nemesis during the early days. The Master therefore adopted a slightly open clubface by further weakening his grip. This ensures that the clubface is always open by a constant angle to the arc. The swing path of the solidly struck shot is inside-square-inside to the line of the forward swing plane which as we know is oriented right of the target line. With a slightly open clubface the resultant ball flight of this swing path is a fade without significant loss of distance. With the stock shot in place, the Master only had to figure out how to deal with the two worst-case scenarios of misfiring Henny Bogan.

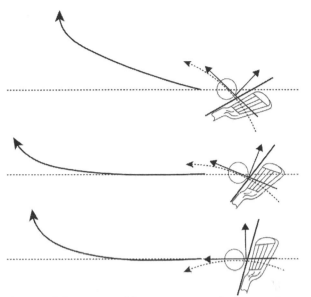

The misses of the top and bottom are relative to the correct path of the solid shot in the center. The inside-out miss of the top yields a push-slice. The solid shot of the center yields a fade. The outside-in miss of the bottom yields a pull-slice.

The first of this is the failure to complete the backswing. When this happens the hips do not coil enough to power the forward swing. The golfer is then forced to take a straight line path to the ball with the arms and the hands. This is an inside-out miss relative to the line of the forward swing plane and will cause a push-slice. The second is the triggering of the forward swing with the shoulders. This over-the-top move makes the forward swing a virtual retrace of the backswing. This is an outside-in miss relative to the line of the forward swing plane and will cause a pull-slice. We can see that in all the possible scenarios, the ball-flight never curves from right to left.

Half a Left Arm

The Master sometimes wished for half a left arm. This Hoganism may appear strange at first but turns completely rational with Henny Bogan. The left arm and the right forearm both transmit the torque to the hands. For maximum efficiency, the clamp or transmission arm should be at right angles to the axis of rotation. In Henny Bogan, the right forearm fulfils this requirement but the left arm does not.

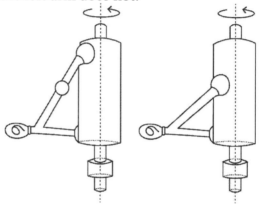

Power in Henny Bogan can be made more efficient by re-moving the length and elbow-joint constraints of the left arm.

First, the left arm's inclination at an acute angle to the axis of rotation is a leakage of power. Second, the left arm is required to be straight and support the right forearm, but it has an elbow joint that can break down the structure of Henny Bogan. An engineer if asked to redesign Henny Bogan would promptly eliminate the left elbow joint, reduce the length of the left arm and bring it lower down the cylinder. This improves the structural integrity of Henny Bogan and also its power efficiency because the left arm now pulls at a less acute angle.

Ben Hogan and Homer Kelley

BEN HOGAN WAS CERTAINLY far ahead of his time when he published *Five Lessons* in 1957. So was Homer Kelly when he published *The Golfing Machine* (*TGM*) in 1969. Hogan's goal was to share the specific techniques for one type of swing. Kelley's goal was to document, through a rather complex system of classification, all the types of swings possible. We know for a fact that Kelley used Hogan as a case study and his two books - *Power Golf* and *Five Lessons* - as reference material. Kelley's work is comprehensive, and yet Hogan's Secret cannot be found in *TGM*. So how does one explain the omission?

In *TGM*, Kelley gives precedence to Geometry over Physics. He says that it is the arms and hands that hold on to and swing the golf club. It is the hands that are used for both aiming and thrusting. The thrust of the hands towards the ball is in a straight line – the Line of Compression - even though their actual path is a circular arc. This is common to all sports that use a hitting or throwing motion. It is therefore the hands that must be monitored throughout the swing. Kelley called this Hands Controlled Pivot. The opposite is Pivot Controlled Hands - monitoring the body instead of the hands. Kelley believed that Pivot Controlled Hands reduced precision and should serve just an intermediate step towards Hands Controlled Pivot. In the final two pages of *TGM*, Kelley describes a circular swing using Pivot Controlled Hands that resembles Hogan's but misses out on one crucial element – the connected structure of Henny Bogan.

In *Five Lessons*, Hogan gives precedence to Physics over Geometry. He says that the body controls the motion of the hands and arms. Now this is true only for the Hogan swing. Its design is such that the body acts as the central pole of a carousel and torques the passive arms and hands around in a circular path by leveraging the ground. This is possible only when the arms and hands are constrained to move in complete sync with the body. Hogan achieved this through Henny Bogan.

The difference between Kelley and Hogan boils down to the prime mover - the power engine of the swing. Kelley's is linear force, Hogan's is rotational force. In a swing where the hands and arms are not always in sync with body rotation, it is the hands that must be monitored. That is because the hands sustain the Line of Compression. Kelley is absolutely right about Hands Controlled Pivot with the single exception of Hogan. Henny Bogan is executed by monitoring the pivot – the feet, hips and shoulders – and not the hands.

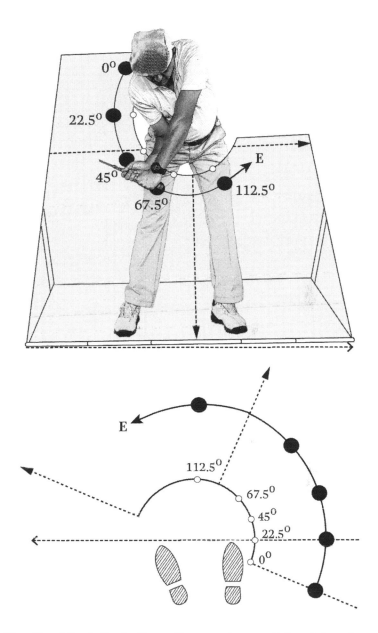

The Hand Path-Body Turn diagram is a useful tool for visual representation of the forward swing.

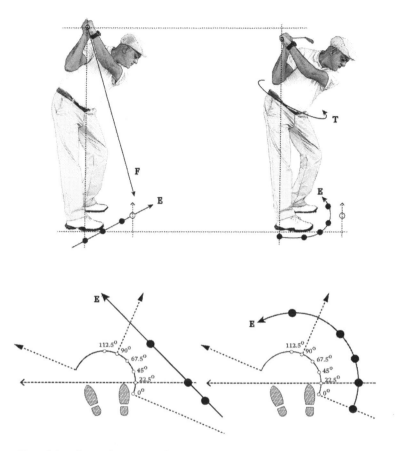

Hand Path-Body Turn diagrams of the golfing machines of Kelley and Hogan. Linear force (F) sustains Kelley's line of compression, rotational force (T) sustains Henny Bogan's circle.

The golfing machines of Homer Kelley and Ben Hogan can be compared graphically. Since there is no such thing as the-one-and-only *TGM* swing, we choose a particular swing that best illustrates Kelley's Line of Compression. We know that lower-body enabled rotation is three discrete steps of $22.5°$ each and independent shoulder rotation is $45°$. We combine this with hand positions *projected on the ground* to arrive at a useful tool for visualizing the forward swing: the Hand Path-Body Turn diagram. The number of hand path points is plotted as per the relationship: (S+N*H) where S=45° shoulder turn, H=22.5° hip turn and N=1, 2 or 3 depending on degrees of lower-body enabled rotation. The hand path is always circular in space but may appear as circular, curvilinear or linear when projected on the ground depending on the swing plane. *Circular* paths indicate perfect arm-body sync; *linear* paths indicate the opposite and *curvilinear* paths somewhere in between. The extension always happens in a *straight* line when the shoulder rotation stalls and the arms go through. The extension is therefore always tangential to the hand path and happens at one of three possible terminal points of shoulder rotation: 67.5 (swinging right), 90 (swinging down the line) and 112.5 degrees (swinging left).

A comparison of the Hand Path-Body Turn diagrams brings out the difference in the shape of hand path, degree of stacking and direction of extension. The linear swing used in this comparison is a model of swinging right while Hogan's circular swing is a model of swinging left. It is possible to swing left or swing down the line using Kelley's paradigm of Hands Controlled Pivot. These are covered in the next two appendices.

One may therefore conclude that Hogan's Secret lies outside the ambit of Kelley's paradigm. To that extent, the One of the Master of Camouflage eluded the Many of the Master of Analysis. I feel privileged and humbled to have learnt from both. It will give me satisfaction if my effort is seen as a small addendum that bridges the work of these two great minds in golf. This book is dedicated to both Masters.

Ben Hogan and
Moe Norman

IT IS AN INTERESTING exercise to compare the Hand Path-Body Turn diagrams of Ben Hogan and Moe Norman because the two are widely regarded as the greatest ball strikers in golf. The two swings do have one thing in common which may well be their common secret of ball-striking greatness: the radius of the circular portion of the Hand Path-Body Turn diagram is defined by the connected right forearm.

Moe used a single plane approach while Hogan had a more orthodox setup. Moe used an extra wide stance to prevent his hips from spinning out because his swing required just two degrees of stacking and not three as in Hogan's swing. Moe's swing was designed to keep the lower body quiet. Hogan designed his to keep the upper body quiet.

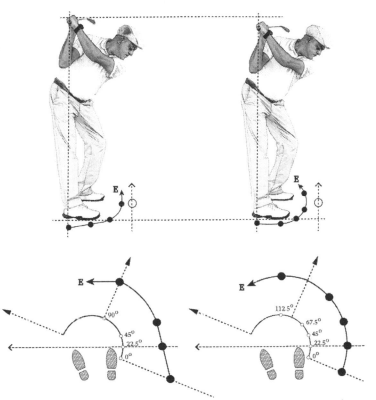

Hand Path–Body Turn diagrams of Moe Norman and Ben Hogan.

In Hogan's backswing, it is the stacking of the right hip-joint that sustains the circular path and flattens the swing plane. In Moe's backswing the hands are allowed to elevate by vertical left-arm action into a higher position at the top. In Moe, the arms are active and used for thrusting. In Hogan, the arms are passive. In Moe, longitudinal acceleration is actively applied at start-down by leveraging against the pivot. In Hogan, longitudinal acceleration is applied passively by the pivot using natural pronation and supination. Moe's extension is down the line while Hogan's is to the left.

Ben Hogan and Swinging Left

IT IS AN OBVIOUS question to ask: what is the difference between the Hogan Swing and other rotational swings that also release to the left? The answer is that the Hogan swing uses the circle of the right forearm while other rotational swings use the circle of the left arm. The right-forearm circle is shorter, shallower and tighter than the left-arm circle.

The right-forearm circle leads to a *stable* release with the clubface always square to the arc in the impact interval. The left-arm circle leads to a *rolling* release where the clubface comes in open but squares up by left-forearm rotation during the impact interval.

A Hogan-like, Pivot-Controlled-Hands swing with passive arms *and* a stable release is possible with the circle of the left arm by starting off with a strong grip at address. This swing must use the deep hip-rotation obtained by three degrees of stacking of lower-body joints: the ankle, knee and hip joints. This is a mandatory requirement if the arms are passive in the forward swing and the release caused by body-rotation.

A stable release without the strong grip is possible by a deliberate supination move before the release interval. But this option is the less preferred one because it involves hand-action in the forward swing.

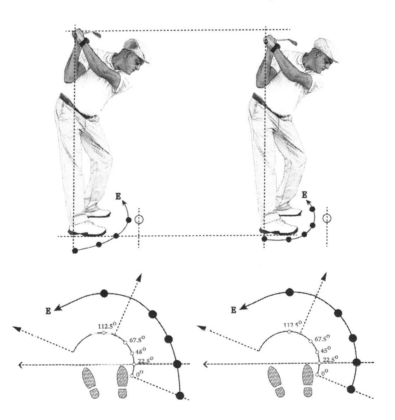

Hand Path–Body Turn diagrams of the left-arm and right-forearm rotational swings.

Acknowledgements

Shawn Clement, the person who taught me golf and many of its secrets. Bamby Randhawa, Gaurav Diwan, C Kumar, R Srinivas and S Sridhar for sharing their golfing knowledge and expertise. The Karnataka Golf Association, the perfect place to play, practice and experiment.

My friend and tournament partner Sriram Srinivasan for his support, ideas and tolerance of my experiments. My friends and playing partners - Sanjay Anand, Irshad Ahmed, Ravi Reddy and Venkat Suri - for their support.

The Managing Committee of KGA for location courtesy of photographs. Irshad Ahmed for modelling courtesy. Venkat Suri and Sanjay Anand for on-course and club house photographs respectively. The kids Rubhav, Ranvit and Ranya for in-house studio photographs.

Mani Nagasubramanian and Yadev for guidance on photography and illustration. Ajoy Chawla for pointing me in the right direction. Elango R for sharing first-hand experience as a published author. Venkat Suri, Dipankar Khashnobish and Ravi Reddy for editorial inputs. Shekhar Verma, Vinay Chandran, Ajay Parikh and Nikhar Khurana - my sounding boards.

My friends Rajesh Rege, Sriram Adukoorie, Alok Ohrie, Durgadutt Nedungadi, Mahesh Jayaram, Dyan Belliappa, Sanjay Verma, Anand Sankaran, Anand Padmanabhan, Tapan Bhat and Suresh Vaswani for keeping me sane.

My wife Shraddha for her unflinching support of this adventure and her patience with my exasperating ways. And our kids, the source of inspiration.

Thank you.

Bibliography

Ben Hogan, Herbert Warren Wind and Anthony Ravielli. *Five Lessons: The Modern Fundamentals of Golf*: Simon & Schuster, Inc.

Homer Kelley. *The Golfing Machine*: The Golfing Machine, LLC.

Scott Gummer. *Homer Kelley's Golfing Machine: The Curious Quest that solved Golf*: Gotham Books.

E.A. Tischler. *Secrets of Owning your Swing*: Self Published.

Shawn Clement: *wisdomingolf.com*

Jim Hardy. *The Plane Truth for Golfers*: McGraw-Hill.

James Dodson. *Ben Hogan - An American Life*: Random House.

Michael Murphy. *Golf in the Kingdom*: Penguin Books.

W. Timothy Gallwey. *The Inner Game of Golf*: Pan Books.

Jeffrey Mann. *perfectgolfswingreview.com*

Geoff Jones. *Slicefixer's Encyclopedia Texarkana*: Self Published

Permissions

Page 9: Quotation reproduced with permission from Time Inc., owners of *Sports Illustrated*.

Page 25: Quotation reproduced with permission from SOFA Inc., copyright owners of the Ed Sullivan Show.

Page 44: Diagram of XPULT catapult kit reproduced with permission from Peloton Systems LLC.

Index

ABOUT THE AUTHOR

The author is a former corporate executive and ex-Vice President at a global IT firm. In 2011, he took a sabbatical after two decades of career pursuit to explore his creative side and to learn to play golf. These twin passions morphed into a single all-consuming labor of love that gave birth to this book. Pradeep has a bachelor's degree in engineering and lives in Bangalore with his wife and three kids.

Made in the USA
Columbia, SC
05 September 2019